GREAT

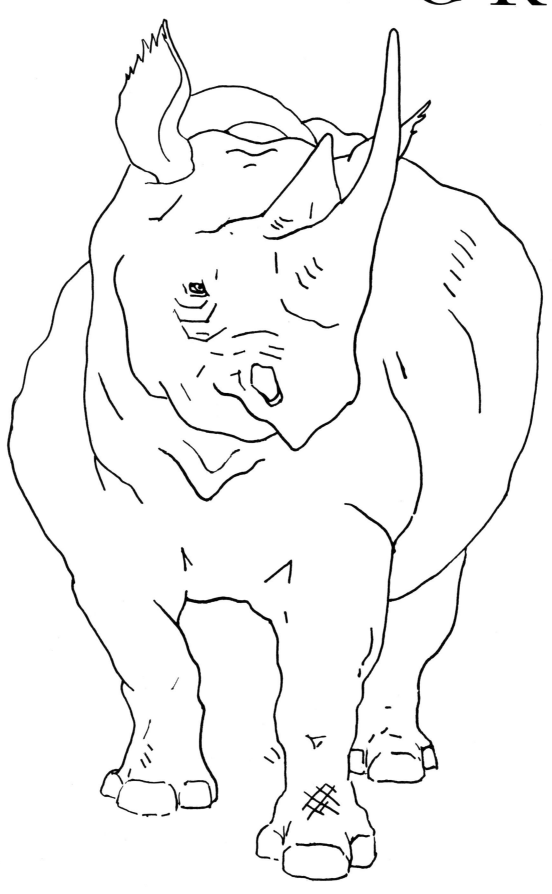

GAME ANIMALS
OF THE WORLD

RUSSELL BARNETT AITKEN, F.R.G.S.

A Giniger Book

THE MACMILLAN COMPANY

This book is affectionately dedicated to my bonnie wife,

Annie Laurie

who is convinced I can do anything she puts her mind to.

This book was designed and produced for
The Macmillan Company,
by The K. S. Giniger Company, Inc.
Manufactured in Italy.

Library of Congress Catalog Card No.: 74-88210

TABLE OF CONTENTS

FOREWORD   6

1. LAND OF SAFARI   8

Out in the Blue 10
The White Hunter 14
A Day on Safari 18
The Nightmare that Walks Like a Pig   27
The Big Four 28
The Black Rhinoceros 30
The Lion 36

The Cape Buffalo 42
The Elephant 48
Glamor Game 58
The Giant Sable Antelope 74
Safari Cars 82
The Bongo 86
Hunting with a Camera 90

2. INDIA & ASIA   92

The Tiger 98
The Marco Polo Sheep 110
Royal Bengals 114

The Gaur 116
The Shikari 123

3. EUROPE   128

The Chamois 134
The Jaeger 135

4. NORTH AMERICA   148

Genesis 150
The Millais Antlers 155
Lend-Lease Animals 164

The Alaskan Guide 166
The Wapiti 172
Carl Rungius 183

5. SOUTH AMERICA   184

Tiger Man 186

FOREWORD

THIS is a book about the original Sport of Kings, the hunting and bagging of big game.

I make no apologies.

In common with many a crowned head of Europe, sundry Maharajas, the Pharaohs of Egypt, and Teddy Roosevelt, I *like* to hunt.

That is why I will listen to no critic of "blood-sports" unless he can prove that he is truly a bona fide vegetarian who has never partaken of a toothsome lamp chop, a sizzling sirloin, or a roast of pork dripping in its own succulent juices. In the hands of an experienced hunter the modern high-velocity rifle is vastly more merciful than are methods used in the abattoirs of civilization.

The compulsion to hunt is as basic a part of man's nature as the mating urge. When the frost is on the ground and antlered bucks are pawing the timbered ridges, it might well take the combined wiles of a Cleopatra, a Helen of Troy, and a Fanny Hill to keep Nimrod home by his hearthside.

That's the way it's been ever since the first hairy cave man used his club on a beast for meat or against a sabre-toothed tiger to save his own hide. It may be latent, but the urge to hunt is inside every man.

What is not generally understood about big game hunters is the fact that the killing, per se, is the least important element. To the sportsman the major thrill is that which comes from outwitting a wary, crafty, or dangerous animal by invading his domain and spooring him up to within proper shooting distance.

The squeezing of the trigger is an anticlimax.

To be successful a hunter needs the instincts and deductive powers of a Scotland Yard detective, stamina equal to that of an Everest climber, the tracking ability of an Ojibway Indian, and the consummate marksmanship of an Olympic medalist.

At heart he is a conservationist.

He kills cleanly and is selective in his choice of game, taking old males no longer useful for breeding. He does not shoot indiscriminately, for to a serious sportsman no trophy at all is better than a poor one.

The big game hunter is a bear for punishment.

Without complaint he will endure backbreaking toil, hikes of marathon distance, and discomforts normally encountered only in jungle warfare. Intense heat and humidity, foul weather, poor food, and assaults by mosquitoes, tsetse flies, fire ants, scorpions, and poisonous snakes are all taken in stride. Although at home he may avoid his own child when it has the mumps, on the trail of a top trophy he will cheerfully risk exposure to malaria, sleeping sickness, hookworm, dysentery and even leprosy.

A dedicated hunter will take a chance on frostbite, pneumonia, heart attack, and the possibility of a broken neck in the pursuit of mountain game whether it be the little chamois of the European Alps, the Walia ibex of Abyssinia, or the great corkscrew-horned *Ovis poli* of the Pamir Plateau.

To get a shot at a tiger he will sit patiently in a leafy *machan* for a dozen grueling hours without moving a muscle—and do it night after night. He will venture into the trackless dunes of the Sahara or the Kalahari from which, if an accident should happen to his White Hunter, he might never return. Galahad in his quest for the Holy Grail never suffered half the tribulations which beset the sportsman who elects to spoor up a bongo in the stinking swamps of the Moyen Congo.

What makes a hunter willing and eager to endure such ordeals?

Primarily it is the unconscious desire to fulfill a boyhood ambition—to slay the savage lion or tiger which had leaped at him from the picture books of his impressionable youth. There is, however, a more compelling reason.

He is a collector.

Just as other people choose to amass stamps, modern art, autographs, vintage automobiles or antique Colt revolvers, *he* collects trophy heads. These he values inordinately because they represent tangible evidence of a successful stalk. They also prove his prowess with a rifle—a prowess which in pioneer days made heroes of Daniel Boone, Kit Carson, and Davy Crockett.

There is more than prowess involved. Life in the bush can bring out the best—or the worst—in any man, and thus poses a challenge, one explored by Ernest Hemingway in *The Short Happy Life of Francis Macomber.*

The neophyte hunter may be a timid chap back home, but facing dangerous game he frequently displays bravery of a caliber which would earn him, in battle, a major decoration. This valor he produces in order to gain the respect of guide or gunbearer, people he in all probability will never see again.

Big-game buffs, of course, have their idols just as do baseball, tennis, and soccer fans. In my time there were four outstanding big game hunters whose feats were hailed around the globe: W.D.M. "Karamojo" Bell, the greatest elephant hunter of them all; Marcus Daly, another case-hardened veteran of the Ivory Trail; Jim Corbett, who tracked down and killed the man-eaters of Kumaon; and J.A. Hunter, guttiest of the East African professionals. It was my privilege to have known them all, and their boots will be rather hard to fill.

A glance at this book will indicate that I am just as keen about animal photography as I am about hunting with a rifle, and I value a fine close-up of dangerous game as much as I do a world record head. In this volume there are 197 of my own photographs. It was my wish to do honor to some of my contemporaries who have also bush-bashed across five continents, and I have included a dozen or so photographs of these dedicated big-game hunters with superb trophies.

I wish to thank the following for lending me the photographs requested: H.I.H. Prince Abdorezza of Iran for his fine pasang; The Maharaja of Jaipur for the photographs of Her Majesty, Queen Elizabeth, with the Duke of Edinburgh's tiger; Mary Hurn for her photograph of the Maharajah of Cooch-Behar; Elgin Gates for photographs of his great *Ovis poli* and Mongolian Argali; Peter Barrett for his color shots of Tito, a mule deer and Axis deer. I want to thank my old and good friend, Sasha Siemel, for his photo of an enormous jaguar bagged with a spear, and Mel Johnson for that of his world record whitetail deer bagged with bow and arrow. My gratitude goes also to Bert Klineburger for his caribou, walrus and buffalo of India trophies; to John LaGarde for Asian ibex and markhor; to Charles Stoll for a big polar bear, —and to David Hasinger for a photo of his Smithsonian-bound tiger, as well as to Frank Delano for a superlative addax.

The big-game hunter worthy of the name is a brave fellow, a gentleman and a sportsman, and his heritage dates back to Ashur-bani-pal, the Hunting King, who ordered carved on the walls of ancient Nineveh his proud boast: "I killed the lion."

I am happy to belong to the fraternity.

RUSSELL BARNETT AITKEN

Tamerlane
Greenwich, Connecticut
August 1, 1968

7

LAND OF SAFARI

ABOVE: Africa is the Land of the Lion, a tawny terror held in high esteem by Masai spearmen, Swazi warriors, and the ancient Pharoahs.

RIGHT: Under Kibo, the snowcapped peak of Mt. Kilimanjaro, a giraffe pauses in its browsing.

AFRICA used to be a very far-off place, too remote for anybody except bona fide explorers and daredevils, a continent familiar to most people only through the films made by Osa and Martin Johnson. Africa by tradition was a land of malaria and of sleeping sickness, of discomfort, great danger, and debilitating heat, and the problems involved getting there and back were formidable. On my earliest safaris when I accompanied my own hunting cars aboard freighters, it frequently required eight weeks to go from the dock in Brooklyn to Kilindini Harbor at Mombasa, and another week's trek to Nairobi and the game country beyond.

Things are different in this jet age. Nairobi is a mere twenty-four hours away from New York's John F. Kennedy International Airport and that time will be slashed radically in the years to come. Modern safari life is quite comfortable, with filtered drinking water, a kerosene refrigerator, fresh linen, and luxury mattresses. The jeep-type vehicles in use can scour wide areas to locate game and there are even light planes available, if your pocketbook can stand it, to deliver you and rifle or camera at a camp already set up out in the blue.

This, of course, is roughing it smoothly. It wasn't always so painless.

In the days of Livingstone and Stanley explorers had to travel on foot and carry sufficient supplies to last many months in the bush—food, medicine, ammunition, tents, clothing, and trading trinkets. Packed into 60-pound bundles or into chop-boxes, all this had to be carried on the heads of several hundred porters. To recruit them—and also to obtain permission for entering East Africa—they first had to sail to Zanzibar. On that spice-scented coral island on the waistline of the world a white bearded potentate lived in exotic splendor and held dictatorial control of the mainland. Swarthy corsairs, sailing in lateen-rigged dhows ahead of the monsoon winds, had come from the Kingdom of Oman to create a domain so powerful that an old proverb boasted: "When the flute is played in Zanzibar, all of Africa east of the lakes must dance."

For over sixty years Nairobi has been the traditional center of safari, catering to a wealthy clientele and arranging every detail of safaris for hunting and photography. Today Nairobi is still supreme but certain other hubs have sprung up to challenge her place. A well-equipped safari might now originate in Livingstone for Barotseland and Botswana. Beira is the jumping-off point for Mozambique; Loanda for Angola; Port Gentil for Gabon; Kampala for Uganda. The Sahara and Ennedi, locales for such rarely bagged beasts as the fleet scimitar oryx, the addax, and the Barbary sheep, are reached by safaris starting at Fort Lamy or Abéché, while Fort Archambault serves as a base of operations when the elusive Lord Derby's eland is the quarry. Bangui, a colorful town with modern air-conditioned hotels, is the place you hop off from when your goal is the green hell of the bongo swamps down in the Moyen Congo. On a small scale, there are now outfitters who will take you into Ethiopia and also the Sudan, regions hitherto inaccessible.

Air travel has revolutionized African hunting. Now it is quite possible to leave home, have an excellent safari, and return home in far less time than it took to just get there fifty years ago. Paradoxically, it often happens that the modern hunter finds far bigger heads than did the early Nimrod who, being forced to travel on foot, could not cover a fraction of the territory possible with proper safari vehicles. The variety of game which can be bagged is limited only by the amount of time available and the size of your wallet.

Africa, the greatest of the continents for hunting and photography, has a charm and lure so strong that an old proverb proclaimed: "He who drinks of Africa's rivers always returns." If he boils the water, that is.

The impala (left), a truly beautiful antelope, still exists in large numbers in East Africa. Gourmets relish the delicate flavor of his tender, tasty venison.

RIGHT: A classic camp near the Mara River in Kenya's Massai District, with tents pitched among the marulas.

OUT IN THE BLUE

YOU can hunt all the way around the world, but the camps that you will remember with the greatest pleasure will be the ones in Kenya. Near the Mara River we pitched our tents high and dry in a grove of fever trees not far from a deep spring-fed brook whose verdant banks were pockmarked by the tracks of bushbuck and duikers that came to drink during the night. In the Masai District, during January and February, the days were always warm and the nights pleasantly cool, and if you needed meat a Tommy gazelle could be dropped not far from the tents, or a short stalk with a shotgun would produce a plump spurfowl, dove, or guinea hen. From this comfortable and delightful base one cruised over a sunbaked plain where a dozen species of game grazed and tiny Tommy totos could be seen bouncing off behind their mothers like four-legged basketballs. A hike up into the dark forests would soon put one onto the spoor of a Cape buffalo bull, a foe worthy of your steel-jacketed ammunition.

With no daily newspapers there were no world crises to upset you and when dusk approached, as it does so quickly, you sipped a sundowner alongside a twinkling campfire, angry at no one. Later, when you crawled under the blankets, you were treated to an evening concert consisting of the chattering of baboons, the distant barks of zebras, and the rasping buzz of the tree hyrax, punctuated on occasion by the cough of a prowling leopard or the snort of a rhino. Sometimes, quite far off, the awesome roar of a lion would intrude into the arrangement, followed by the ghoulish cackles of slinking slope-backed hyenas quite near the camp.

The regular background music in this nocturnal symphony was generally rendered by a million or two nonunion insect musicians, some shrill, some softly muted, with various interpolated solos offered by bird insomniacs and by ubiquitous monkeys up in the treetops. The strident melody created by the many voices of the African night lingers in one's memory forever.

The gestation period for a giraffe is 14½ months. Three days after birth the toto can bounce happily across the plains and at six months will be a fully active ruminant. When grown its tongue will measure eighteen inches long and can pluck the tender top leaves off an acacia tree.

Giraffes, zebras, trees, and thornbush have a habit of arranging themselves into tapestry patterns as if a stage-manager had called directions. The giraffe's keen vision, from his high vantage point, makes him an ideal sentinel, ready to sound the alarm if a lion or hunter approaches

Australian Frank Bowman, one of the best of the post-World War II white hunters. He trained several young apprentices such as Harry Selby, who is now a veteran.

THE WHITE HUNTER

SHORTLY after the turn of the century a new profession came into existence in East Africa: the white hunter, a stalwart fellow who shepherds you out into the blue among the wildest of wild beasts and brings you back alive. His clan has been so glamorized by a combination of Hemingway, Ruark, and Hollywood that a lot of clients, especially female ones, expect to be met on arrival by a dashing chap six feet tall with broad shoulders, an amorous leer in his eye, a toothpaste-ad smile, and a beer glass clutched in his hand.

Very few real-life professional hunters could double for film stars and some of them are types which you might pass on the street without a second glance. The able ones are anything but flamboyant, are often of medium stature, and many are almost painfully shy. But don't let appearances mislead you. The probabilities are rather good that they were killing buffalo and tracking rhino at an age when you were still in knee pants and pimples.

In his adopted land his salary is considered a good one—but he earns every penny. Besides having to be a diplomat, since the veneer of civilization vanishes rather rapidly in the bush, he also has to be a doctor of sorts, a master mechanic, and a raconteur. He chauffeurs his clients into wild and even dangerous country and supervises the setting up of a camp far more elaborate than he would want if he were out on his own. He mixes drinks at sundown with the aplomb of a 21 Club bartender, and plans exotic menus to be prepared over a campfire by a native chef whose grandfather probably ate people. He finds and spoors up the game, and by tradition keeps his temper when his tenderfoot bobbles the shot at some target which might possibly be a record-smashing rarity. His tact is remarkable, his patience boundless, and his courage legendary. The credo of the veteran white hunter is short and sweet: You never leave a wounded beast behind or come back to camp with a dead customer.

Philip Percival, dean of all the white hunters of East Africa, veteran of over fifty years of safari. In 1909 he turned professional after guiding ex-President Teddy Roosevelt on a successful lion hunt on the Athi Plains.

Dave Lunan, one of Kenya's top white hunters, has to be booked a couple of years in advance. In the film *King Solomon's Mines* he had to drop a tusker at thirty paces, and a rhino at ten in *The Snows of Kilimanjaro*.

The brindled gnu or common blue wildebeeste (*Connochaetes taurinus*) was once known as the "horned horse". He is one of Africa's most numerous grass-eaters and is often mistaken for the Cape buffalo by the tyro on his first hunt.

Over 100,000 wildebeeste roam the Serengeti and regularly migrate to certain traditional calving grounds. They look as if they were made up of spare parts of cows and ponies and are readily recognizable by their clownish caperings.

A DAY ON SAFARI

Each day of safari is a spin of the wheel of fortune, for nobody can say what lies over a ridge or lurks in the gallery forest nearby.

THE swish of the mosquito net *chandalua* being lifted wakes you on a typical day of safari. A deep but gentle voice greets you, saying in Swahili, "Tea, Bwana," and a tray is plunked down on the bedside table near the head of your cot. By the flickering yellow light of a kerosene lantern your wristwatch says it is only five-thirty and although you are not addicted to *chai* at such an unholy hour you grab it as you reach for your woolen socks, clammy khakis, and a cardigan sweater.

Breakfast, partaken gratefully alongside a roaring fire, shakes the sleep out of your system and after a quick check of guns and ammunition you wrap yourself in a trench coat and muffler and climb aboard the safari car. In the back the tracker and gunbearers huddle like quick-frozen zombies who will defrost later in the heat of the sun.

Beneath a black velvet curtain stippled with stars the car bulldozes its tortuous way through the high grass, sopping wet with dew, plunges boldly down into a wooded donga, splashes across a tiny creek and lurches up the far side to emerge onto the plains as daylight begins to seep into the world of the veldt. The crimson spears of the dawn silhouette a herd of giraffe racking along the horizon in slow motion, and directly ahead of the radiator cap long lines of zebra, kongoni, and wildebeeste race madly across in a suicidal game of their own invention.

Beyond them, spread among the groves of table-top acacias, Tommy gazelles by the score graze complacently, tails wagging like berserk metronomes. Off to the right, from a patch of wait-a-bit, a worried wart hog sow, her tusks sweeping upward in a Kaiser Bill mustache, gallops off with five little piglets trailing with such precision that it reminds you of a bantam locomotive and train, the last small grunter—covered in red mud—being the caboose.

Half a mile farther on, off to the left in a thicket of whistling thorn, a large gray rock suddenly begins to walk and becomes a cow rhino, her front horn not much bigger than a banana. Approaching closer we shoot her—on film—as she gallops off.

By now it has become a land shot to the core with sunlight and having emerged from your cocoon of top-

coat you are swatting tsetse flies as they probe at the back of your neck. Overhead a bateleur eagle, the ultimate in streamlined design, soars in an effortless glide. Far above him, mere specks in the blue, several vultures seem suspended as they hover in perpetual patrol, the death watch of the African skies.

It is late afternoon when the Lumbwa tracker taps on the side of the car and points a brown finger to the south. His eyes, equal to any pair of six-power binoculars, have spotted game moving near the fringe of the forest, and the white hunter takes one quick look and says "Buff!" This is the brute that you are keen to bag, this is the breed that has crippled and killed natives and professional hunters and luckless amateurs, and your heart starts pounding a little harder than usual.

This is it. This is what you have traveled ten thousand miles to do and now that you are dismounting from the car, well hidden from the herd, you begin to wonder if it was such a good idea after all. Reaching into the car you take out the heavy gun, a .470 caliber, knowing that it has the best stopping power.

The white hunter leads the procession, his own rifle slung over his shoulder. You are next in line, with your heavy artillery, and behind you a tracker. City life seems far behind and you know that you are truly on safari.

Cresting cautiously over a ridge you discover that you are within sight of a sentry cow and, dropping to a prone position, you snake along as your white hunter is doing, placing the rifle ahead of you and dragging yourself up to it by your elbows, inchworm fashion. Hidden by high grass, you are now near enough to catch the sweet cattle smell and notice green chlorophyll slime on the blunt black muzzle of the closest Cape buffalo. The spread of the horns is impressive, as is the thick helmet of boss, rived like oak bark. Although they all look desirable to you, your mentor—after a careful survey—says that none is of trophy quality and so you retreat as carefully as you came. You haven't fired a shot as yet, but it doesn't matter because you know that when you are old and gray you will still recall the heady thrill of that stalk and your first close-up glimpse of the lethal Mbogo.

". . . you will always recall your first glimpse of the lethal Mbogo" — the husky Cape buffalo.

When nomad Somalis move camp the patient cows and camels
are loaded with the *gurgi* (tent) and household effects.
Camels, which constitute the Somali's wealth, can graze
four hours each day and are ridden only in emergencies.

The zebra is Africa's most typical animal, existing in a variety of stripes in many different areas. A nasty-tempered species, stallions bite and kick each other in deadly earnest. The zebra, alarmed, barks like a fox terrier.

The eland (above) is the largest antelope in the world, weighs almost a ton and can vault over the tops of some thorn trees like a steeplechaser. The amusing steinbok, opposite, is a pygmy antelope as small as a fox terrier.

22

A medium-size buck, the impala is the most acrobatic of all the African antelopes. When alarmed, he takes off in astonishing leaps, spanning as much as thirty feet as he clears the tops of the scrub thorn trees.

The cheetah *(Acinonyx jubatus)* or "hunting leopard" is a catlike animal with nonretractile claws like a dog. Nonaggressive toward humans, he is remarkably fast for a short sprint and can run down a gazelle.

THE NIGHTMARE THAT WALKS LIKE A PIG

THE poor man's rhino is what they call the wart hog (*Phacochoerus aethiopicus*). His keg-sized head would look more at home on a Chinese dragon. Small and evil red-rimmed eyes are set high in wrinkled dark pouches like raisins stuck in a bun, flanked below by a brace of bulbous rubbery wens which give him his name. His hide, naked as a Chihuahua's, is trimmed with a horsy mane and a buggy-whip disguised as a tail sprouts from his fat behind. There is nothing funny about the tusks, great curving canines that would shame a wild boar of Europe. There are two sets of them nested together, the big upper pair being used as shovels for digging up tubers and also as whetstones for the razor-sharp fighting ones below. A world record pair from Abyssinia taped a fantastic 26 and 27 inches on outside curve.

THE BIG FOUR

ABOVE: The lion is becoming scarce in East Africa but is holding his own in the Sudan where he climbs trees with the agility of a leopard.

RIGHT: Second only to the elephant in size is the white, or square-lipped, rhinoceros, whose massive hunp and blunt snout immediately distinguish him from his commoner black cousin.

THOUSANDS of books have been written on Africa and its big game and most of them have glorified a grim quartet of beasts which hunters call "The Big Four"—elephant, rhinoceros, lion, and Cape buffalo. It is not surprising that these animals, three hulking heavyweights and one snarling mass of muscles, teeth, and claws, should earn a nasty reputation when you consider that countless corpses lie in lonely bush graves because of them. Many hunters died in the early days when percussion firearms were not infallible, but today others are being killed in spite of bone-shattering express weapons and specialized magnums which hit with the wallop of a .50 caliber machine-gun bullet. The vitality of African game is so incredible that a favorite admonition to a client by his white hunter is "Clobber him again. It's the dead ones that get up and kill you!"

There is scarcely a professional hunter who hasn't had trouble, lots of it, with various members of the Big Four, often without provocation.

Too many tenderfeet are prone to think of a rhino as a big, blubbery boob when in fact he might represent a vindictive mass of malice. Major Stigand, a famous big-game hunter, was gored to within an inch of his heart but survived. A case-hardened veteran East African professional hunter, old Bwana Cottar, was plenty tough but not as tough as the cow rhino which killed him near Barakitabu. Any brash beginner who thinks he can sidestep a charge of an angry rhino had better make sure, first, that his life insurance is paid up.

The African lion, five hundred pounds of brawling brawn, fools a lot of first-timers on safari because he looks like a good-natured tomcat as he suns himself on an anthill or wanders, well fed, across the plains. A lot of chastened hunters know better. Old explorer Dr. David Livingstone, hunting lions with a Bechuana tribe, was badly mauled by a lion which had been wounded and which attacked him as he was recharging his muzzle loader. The guttiest of white hunters thinks twice before starting into high grass after a wounded lion—and when he does his favorite weapon is a 12-gauge shotgun loaded with buckshot. At close range its concentrated pattern will blow Simba's noggin clean off, it is true, but only an idiot worries about ruining a trophy head when the animal to which it is attached is trying to ruin him.

As for the Cape buffalo, tales of terrors perpetrated by this bully boy of the bushveldt are legion. He has a mean little trick of circling on his backtrack to wait in the shadows for the hunter, and when he declares war there'll be no armistice. He'll toss you, rip you with his horns, trample you to mush; and he's even been known to lick a man's leg to the bone with his rasp-like tongue. Hit in a nonvital spot he requires a lot more lead to put him down for the count, and many a white hunter is terrified of Mbogo.

Yet these three—the rhino, lion, and Cape buffalo—are tame stuff compared to the African elephant. The elephant is the most animal you can hunt in the world. He's a lot more than most neophytes want when they've found him. He's a hell of a lot more than they want after he finds *them*.

Deerhunters are familiar with buck fever, a mental state characterized by a nervous panic.

Multiply it by a thousand and you'll get a sketchy idea of the jitters that rattle a man when his white hunter shoves him up close enough to fox trot with a monster that looks as big as Grant's Tomb and is potentially more dangerous than a tornado. Many veterans of the ivory trail had near-fatal encounters with Tembo—Neumann, Selous, Finaughty, Marcus Daly, and Major Pretorious, and so did Carl Akeley and fresh-from-the-White House Teddy Roosevelt.

Not all elephants are aggressive. Basically the beast is cheerful, trustworthy, loyal, helpful, friendly, and courteous—but not necessarily to big-game hunters and brash photographers.

THE BLACK RHINOCEROS

In the headlights of a safari jeep (above) two rhinos fight a grim duel, using their horns to parry the vicious thrusts and jabs of the foe.

RAYMOND Hook, one of Kenya Colony's more colorful characters, was once asked if he considered the rhinoceros dangerous.

"No more so," said Hook, "than a drunken omnibus driver in a London fog."

That fairly well describes the big black rhino of Africa, which can be timid as a titmouse or as terrible as a typhoon. A mature bull, which might live to an age of forty or better, weighs almost three tons, stands five and a half feet at the shoulder and measures twelve feet in length. When angry, which can be often, he will attack anything of any size, shape, or color, and in Kenya's early days one actually attempted to bulldoze a locomotive off the track when it tooted at him in the wrong key. For all his bulk he is nimble as a fat man on a dance floor, turning in as short an area as a polo pony. Though his eyesight is poor, his high-frequency hearing and phenomenal sense of smell make up for the deficiency. He travels on regular trails through the bush and when undisturbed retires daily to his own private latrine.

A crude brute with a stout snout and a short snort, the rhino has a face that would stop a clock; but his reputation, his size, and his fabulous horn have been responsible for luring countless hunters to Africa.

His horn has been his undoing. It is actually not horn at all but really a mound of agglutinated hair which is fastened firmly to his skin but not to his thick skull. Call it what you like, it has resulted in his persecution for untold centuries. In the Middle Ages, around the time the Borgias were specializing in lethal cocktails, someone decided that a cup made from the horn of a rhinoceros would shatter if a poisonous liquid were put into it. Everybody wanted one and eventually the price reached 1500 crowns, roughly $3,000 at current rates. Even the Pope purchased one, paying 12,000 pieces of gold for it. It was also extremely popular in far-off China, where it was rumored to be a potent aphrodisiac when reduced to a powder. His horn was also used by Zulus as a haft for their battle axes, and in the 19th century the Boers made sjambok whips from his hide. Now his tribe is doomed unless more protection is given it, for he is a bewildered beast edging closer and closer to extinction. When his great dreadnought hulk has disappeared from forest and from plain, Africa will never be quite the same again, for the animal was an integral part of a wild and enchanting land.

Virtually all rhinos have suppurating sores just back of the front leg, as on the rhino cow above, and tick birds tear at the raw flesh of these wounds in a ghoulish way. The charging rhino opposite tried to tip over my car just a split second later, having snorted out of a thorn clump.

The white, or Burchell's rhinoceros, (*Ceratotherium simum*) is, next to the elephant, the largest land mammal extant. Its head, with its blunt truncate muzzle, is shaped like a sack of cement and it appears to be hiding a football under its skin at the crest of the spine. It is a grazer.

The black rhinoceros (*Diceros bicornis*) in comparison to the white species, appears almost streamlined. While the square-lipped species has a much longer and heavier horn, it is almost square at the base. The black rhino's upper lip is prehensile and somewhat resembles a parrot's beak.

THE LION

A male lion with heavy mane (right) was scarce even sixty years ago. Very few animals in Africa are as dangerous as an angry lioness (above) crouched and ready to charge at lightning speed.

MARCUS Daly, one of the toughest of all the old-time professional hunters, confessed that it took many encounters before he found the courage to stand steady and meet the awesome charge of an angry lion.

Winston Churchill, in his early days as a Boer War correspondent, called Simba "wicked and cowardly," an undiplomatic thing to say about the symbol of his own Empire and a long way from being accurate.

The lion is dynamite to play around with because he can make himself look docile as a domestic tabby.

He isn't.

In a game park, where he has become used to motorcars and handouts, he'll let you drive up within ten yards or less. You might even get the impression that he is ignoring you completely.

That's what *you* think.

Make a menacing move, or step out of the car, and the amber orbs dilate until they're bigger than poker chips. The head dips down imperceptibly and the tufted tail starts to lash in a frenzy. Suddenly it snaps up, stiff as a broomstick, and you're in real trouble.

With all his 450 pounds of brawn, the animal is capable of crouching flat in a hummock that couldn't hide a hare. He charges at rocket speed with mouth open wide as a cave and trimmed with yellow teeth only slightly smaller than railroad spikes. If your bullet misses a vital spot he can absorb enough lead to sink a scuba diver—and steel tapes have proven that a lion can span 40 feet at a leap in full gallop.

The deep-seated dread of the beast as a man-eater dates back to imperial picnics in Roman arenas where the lion's diet consisted mainly of fresh Christians. One could hardly expect the starved brutes to look a gift martyr in the face when he was the only entree on the menu.

Lions become man-eaters sometimes when they can no longer catch and kill game, so they turn to man as a slower, more abundant viand. They may also get a hankering for human flesh as a result of certain tribes leaving their dead and dying relatives in the forest for the hyenas to finish off. The most famous of all man-eaters was the pair of lions which halted construction of the Kenya-Uganda railroad in the last days of the 19th Century. These maneless marauders, stealthy as stoats, devoured helpless Hindu coolies by the dozen, garnished them with fat Parsee stationmasters, and for dessert broke into sleeping cars to gobble up white passengers. The grisly reign of terror was only ended when Col. J. H. Patterson finally

bagged them, an event important enough to be announced, in London, in the middle of a debate in the House of Lords.

More recently there was the man-eater of Mikindani, a fearsome brute of the Southern Tanganyika thornbush, who ran up a score of 380 victims before he was slain.

Fortunately for the safari business, few lions fancy the human race as a steady diet; 99 percent prefer to eat a fat zebra rather than make a meal of a popcorn-fed Yank or a Britisher fattened on austerity and bubble-and-squeak. It's the liberal-minded 1 percent that take the monotony out of lion hunting.

Sixty years ago, in the Kruger Park, a game ranger named Wolhuter killed an aggressive member of those 1-percenters by stabbing it repeatedly with a knife held in his left hand. The reason he wasn't able to use his right hand was because it was in the lion's mouth at the time.

An occupational hazard of safari is the possibility of having Simba grunting and prowling around your tent late at night. It happened to me up on the northwestern border of Northern Rhodesia (now Zambia) when a big hungry lion invaded camp and tried to snatch my best Kaonde-Ila boy out of his bedroll.

Being the Big Bwana, I was expected by tradition to grab flashlight and rifle and sally forth bravely into the yellow grass in my pajamas. I did, but a motivating factor was the fact that he'd return to sample me next. When I finally managed to shine the brute's eyes and slap him with a slug, my teeth were chattering "Rock of Ages" in ragtime and it wasn't because of the temperature. That ornery lion pegged out at over ten feet and had looked bigger than a Kodiak brownie to me over my wobbling gunbarrel.

Twenty years ago, in Kenya's Mara River country, I was stalking a big herd of Cape buffalo in dense forest and was just lining up my sights on a fine bull when some sixth sense made me turn around. While I'd been busy stalking the herd, I'd been stalked myself by a whopper of a lioness who was crouched and ready to spring less than twenty yards away. As soon as she saw that I had spotted her she uttered a loud "WHOOF" and zoomed into the thick bush, barged into a cranky buffalo cow, and started a stampede that very nearly reduced me to hamburger. Considering the direction of the wind, there is no question that I was the target of the lioness, and it will help you understand why I never downgrade the lion.

After a night of nonstop romance a lioness and her paramour lie exhausted in the shade, the male keeping an eye peeled for danger. He might live to fifteen if unmolested and she will average four cubs to a litter. The lioness does all game killing, preferring a fat zebra. (opposite)

Vultures huddled in a tree at dawn usually mean that there is a lion on a kill nearby, a tip-off for the eager hunter.

A lion's kill is often made in the vicinity of water, so that the insatiable thirst generated by a night of gorging on fresh meat can be quenched quickly without the bother of taking a long walk in the broiling sun.

A classic dark-maned lion of Tanganyika walks along a game trail on his way to water. Such a mature male might weigh 450 pounds and tape nine feet ten inches from tip of nose to tail tuft, a superlative trophy.

THE CAPE BUFFALO

Three fine old Cape buffalo bulls with trophy horns (above) are a rare sight. Bulls such as these and the loner opposite might weigh close to a ton, being heavy boned and solid of body.

BASICALLY a Cape buffalo is a shy heavyweight that will avoid man like the plague, but push him around and he becomes hell-on-wheels with a supercharger. A wounded one is the sort of critter that gives a white hunter instant gray hair. Such a bull, bloody minded, is a master at circling to wait alongside his tracks in ambush, silent as the grave and blacker than the surrounding shadows. When the hunter passes, eyes to the ground and intent on the blood spoor, the buffalo rushes out from behind to hook him on his mighty horns.

The bull that attacks without provocation is generally an old rogue forced from herd and harem and in an understandably nasty mood because of it—or it is an animal which has been previously wounded by a bullet, arrow, or spear and is out to get even with mankind without regard to race, creed, or color.

That's when he handles man-killing with all the ardor of a weasel at work in a henhouse. Unlike the *toro* of the Spanish bullring, a Cape buffalo attacks with head up and baleful red-rimmed eyes glued solidly on his target. Any matador stupid enough to try a *veronica* on this outsize wild ox would find himself shish-kebab'd in two shakes. For variety, in the middle of his mayhem, he likes to crush a man beneath his big splayed hooves and sometimes, maddened by the odor of salty human perspiration, he'll use a raspy tongue to lick a helpless hunter's flesh clear to the bone. I have had to stop a charging buffalo at 12 yards and it is not my personal idea of a picnic.

The big Cape buffalo bull (opposite) is a rogue, forced from the herd by a younger bull and in a nasty mood as a result. I bagged him with camera only. The enormous bull above, with 53½-inch horns, I killed while on safari in the Masai District with white hunter Dave Lunan.

Unlike the *toro* of the Spanish bullring, the Cape buffalo attacks with head up and eyes zeroed in on his target. He has killed and crippled scores of professional hunters and is a great game animal. The whopper opposite I shot some 20 years ago with Frank Bowman very high up on Mt. Kenya.

THE ELEPHANT

THE oldest argument in any big-game hunting group is: Which is the most dangerous animal in the world? The most dangerous animal in the world, so far as I am concerned, is the one which when angry can do the most damage. By that criterion no beast can even be mentioned in the same breath as the African elephant.

With him trouble comes by the ton.

Hunting this modern mammoth makes every other type of shooting seem duller than dishwater. In quest of a pair of trophy tusks you creep up to a herd, checking the wind at every yard gained. One minute things are quiet as a nightclub at noon.

Then the breeze shifts.

Elephants stop feeding and start fidgeting. Alarm signals rumble in their bellies. Ears big as beach-umbrellas open out into great cups to trap the faintest foreign sound. Trunks stiffen as if at a command and go aloft to oscillate in mid-air like a covey of nervous cobras.

Suddenly a sentry cow screams.

Simultaneously the thornbush all around you erupts with beasts bigger than Tiger Tanks and fully as lethal. You are in the eye of the hurricane, the hub of an earth-shaking stampede, and your double-barrel express rifle has shrunk to popgun dimensions.

Later, in retrospect, you may claim that you were not afraid. And you'll be a liar.

I have hunted the African elephant to almost every corner of Africa where they roam and I'm not ashamed to admit that it is one animal which makes the roof of my mouth go cottony dry every time I approach to proper distance for the brain shot—20 yards or less.

And I am not alone.

I've known half a dozen oldtime ivory hunters who have been in the same boat. Sooner or later they met one particular elephant who drove them into such a state of sheer fear that they had to go out and kill an elephant—any elephant—in a hurry or they knew they'd never track his tribe again.

It wasn't whimsy on their part. When it comes to malice, murder, and mayhem, Tembo takes the palm.

This six-ton monster wages total war. It's useless to climb a tree because if he can't shake you out of it like a coconut he'll trumpet for a brace of pals and they'll push it down.

If you're hiding in the reeds and he can't locate you, he'll rip up a sapling and beat the grass until he flushes you out like a quail.

If you've wounded him in a nonvital spot, he may wait in the bushes to grab you with a long, flexible trunk which is half python and half vacuum cleaner.

If he catches you, *pax vobiscum.*

Consider yourself lucky if he bashes your head in against a rock the way a mongoose cracks an egg. At least it's over in a hurry that way. Some elephants enjoy kneeling on a man while they run a tusk through his tripes.

Others, grape-treaders at heart, feel that the best method is to stomp the victim to a frothy pudding under a foot twice the width of a bar-stool cushion. Another fairly popular technique involves curling the trunk into a pile driver. Three wallops is par for the course, after which you can be folded up like a napkin. A few of the more acrobatic pachyderms favor rolling on you like a dog on a dead fish.

Probably the oddest unprovoked brush with a tusker happened to the late, great Carl Akeley, taxidermist and naturalist. He was minding his own business high up in the forests of Mt. Kenya when, out of nowhere, he was suddenly bracketed by a big pair of tusks to which the original owner was still attached. In a reflex action the aged explorer grabbed an ivory shaft with each hand, which saved him from being skewered on the next thrust. The mad bull battered him to the ground, smashing him with its trunk and reducing his nose to a pulp and tearing one cheek open to expose the teeth. Only the hard ground prevented the tusks from digging deeper or Akeley would have been mashed to a pancake. Eventually the berserk beast left him for dead, a diagnosis almost correct.

In Zambia a dozen years ago, I saw an old touring car which had been used by a couple of elephant poachers. They had wounded a big herd bull but their shots had been hasty ones, fired in panic, and hadn't stopped him as he swung toward them. One he grabbed with his trunk, dashing the man's head against the nearest tree, while the other, with a jammed gun, had run off in terror. The car, when I looked at it a few weeks later, had been pounded, smashed, and bulldozed by that angry elephant into a flat solid mass roughly the shape of a sardine tin. It was almost as good a job as they do in wrecking yards where giant machines crush a chassis into a nearly rectangular pig of scrap metal.

There are two sides to every coin. A majority of Africa's veteran white hunters would agree that the greatest elephant hunter to ever set foot there was W.D.M. "Karamojo" Bell, a Scotsman who first landed in 1897 and spent several decades on the ivory trail. In that time he killed well over 2,000 tuskers, many of them with the .276 and even the little .256.

If anybody should have had trouble with elephants, it would have been Bell using these pipsqueak calibers on such massive monsters, and yet in the course

OPPOSITE: An elephant enjoys a bath and will stay in a pool for hours, using his trunk as a hose. A strong swimmer, he can cross rivers and has been known to walk on the bottom with the tip of his trunk above water as a snorkel.

of our many discussions on big game he insisted that in all his years on the ivory trail, including those five when he was the only white man in the virtually unknown wilds of Uganda, only once was he charged by an elephant. He had been trailing a herd when a cow, extremely belligerent, barred his way and made what he thought was merely a demonstration. Instead she kept pressing the charge home and finally, with much regret, he killed her. The reason, as he soon found out, was that the retreating herd in their haste had trampled on her small calf, which Bell found several yards ahead of him, dead, in the reeds.

How is it, you will ask, that Bell experienced so little trouble with the elephant when almost all the other professionals such as Neumann, a contemporary, and Selous, of much earlier vintage, had very narrow escapes from death while hunting them? I don't think it was because many of Bell's beasts had never heard the sound of a rifle and therefore did not associate it with danger, because that was equally true in the case of Selous.

The answer to this riddle probably lies in Bell's

phenomenal accuracy with any rifle but particularly with his pet weapon, the little .256. A high degree of proficiency didn't just happen, however. He liked to carry this one himself and during the daily hikes while spooring up tuskers would stop to aim the rifle at a tree or a rock or at a passing antelope or zebra. Sitting in front of his tent on the shore of a lake, in the evening, he would shoot at cormorants as they flew over him and within a short time managed to kill a high percentage with a rifle.

At the height of his success at ivory hunting Bell was accompanied by an average of 150 porters and all of them loved to eat meat—lots of it. To get fresh meat, Bell once sneaked into the middle of a herd of Cape buffalo and dropped 23 of them stone dead with a .22 Hi-power rifle loaded with soft-nose bullets. It was the same way with elephant. I doubt if any other hunter has ever known animal anatomy as did Bell. He knew exactly how to locate and penetrate the brain of the big beast from any angle. His best day's kill added up to a phenomenal 19 bull tuskers, an accomplishment without parallel.

The angry bull (above) rushed out of a donga, without provocation, and chased my car, and failing to catch it proceeded to demolish an anthill—tough as concrete—to bits.

The big bull (right) tried to kill me without any reason, but a trickle of dark fluid from a gland between eye and ear indicated that he was suffering the madness of *musth.*

For the big-game hunter or photographer there is no thrill in the world to match the one you get when you approach to within twenty yards of the African bull elephant, the most dangerous animal on the face of the earth. In his own domain (right) he is peaceable; on the warpath he is a terror.

One of the loveliest sights in Africa is a herd swinging through towering daum-palms and thornbush on the banks of the classic Uaso Nyiro River in Kenya. Opposite, a female with unusually fine tusks scouts ahead of her small herd.

By sheer tonnage the hippopotamus *(Hippopotamus amphibius)* ought to rate along with the Big Four, but this grotesque tub of blubber is not considered a sporting trophy and is rarely molested. It can walk on the bottoms of lakes and rivers, sunburns easily in spite of 2-inch thick skin, and sweats a wine-red mucus. A big bull might weigh three tons.

Not large enough in body to qualify as a full-fledged member of the Big Four, the leopard *(Felis pardus)* is pound-for-pound as dangerous as any animal in the world. Mainly nocturnal, most leopards are shot over a bait late in the afternoon from a blind nearby. They are powerful enough to haul a zebra up as high as twenty feet off the ground.

GLAMOR GAME

Rated by many as the most beautiful big-game animal in the world, the sable antelope (*Hippotragus niger*) is a bold and brave antelope who defends himself ably with scimitar horns.

OF the many species of antelopes in Africa, a few stand out as star attractions, animals so extremely handsome and rare that they stir the imagination of both the hardened veteran and the eager amateur. One of the most coveted trophies is the sable antelope bull (pictured opposite), a magnificent beast of noble stature whose coat ranges in color from medium chocolate to glossy black. Hard to find, hard to stalk, and not easy to kill, he rates as one of the choicest of game animals in existence. He was discovered in 1836 by a British officer on leave from India, Captain William Cornwallis Harris, who saw a fine bull in the Cashan Mountains of what is now the Northern Transvaal. So entranced was he by the sight of this unknown animal that he abandoned an elephant hunt to pursue it. When finally cornered it charged him twice and when it lay dead he was delighted by its size, decorative mask, and heavy scimitar-shaped horns. His partner, equally impressed, ventured an opinion. "I think," he said, "that this sable antelope will receive the admiration of the world."

He was, of course, correct—and for almost eighty years the animal, called Harrisbuck for quite a while, had no rival. Then, in 1913, H.F. Varian discovered a new and grander species, *Hippotragus niger variani*, a beast almost identical except for less white on the mask and awe-inspiring horns which sweep in great arcs back toward the rump, heavy horns with massive rings.

The habitat of this superb beast, the giant sable antelope, is a small area of wooded tableland at an altitude of 3,700 feet in the Luando Reserve and Cangandala area of Angola. By the last count of investigators for the World Wildlife Fund, between 500 and 700 of the animals still thrive under protection.

Today this elegant and rare beast is fully protected. So startling is the beauty of a properly mounted record-class specimen that a great number of sports-men rate him the No. 1 trophy of the entire world, surpassing even the fabulous Marco Polo sheep of the Asian Pamirs.

Ranking high among the glamor game is the greater kudu, an antelope with corkscrew horns, the one which Hemingway had so much trouble finding in *The Green Hills of Africa*. Unlike the hot-tempered sable, the kudu is dangerous only if he falls on you, and for all his bulk he takes off over scrub bush like an impala. When alarmed he barks like a dog and knows how to lay his spiral horns flat along his withers so that he is able to plunge through very dense thorn thickets with ease. His beige coat is trimmed with vertical stripes of chalky white and a distinctive white chevron spans the bridge of his patrician nose.

The inyala, called by Zulus "the shifty one," is a cousin of the kudu and lives in dense bush in Mozambique, Zululand, and may still exist in remote areas of Malawi.

South Africa boasts another fine trophy not easily taken, the gemsbok of the Kalahari, largest and finest of the oryx family. Not many mounted heads of African game outshine that of a big gemsbok bull with long tapering spearlike horns and dappled beige and black-and-white mask in bold design. This tough and truculent antelope roams the arid, windswept karroo, the semi-desert flanking the micaceous dunes of the vast Kalahari. So adept is he at wielding his rapier horns that even the lion hesitates to attack him.

Going north into Abyssinia, we find it the home of two candidates for the top glamor group. Foremost is the husky walia ibex found in the mountains of Simien, a high-altitude beast of 260 pounds with a grizzled chestnut-brown coat fading to lighter coloration. He is currently protected, as he should be, poaching by local natives having reduced his tribe badly. Another choice Abyssinian species is the mountain nyala, almost as large as the kudu but with lyre-

In a tsetse-fly infested patch of sunbaked Zambian bushveldt, this pair of sable antelope forage. If wounded, a sable bull will sometimes attack a man.

To many hunters the greater kudu (opposite) is the ultimate in perfection due to his elegant bearing, magnificent spiral horns, and the stylish white stripping of his beige coat. He is gentle but wary.

Two fine greater kudu bulls roam the bush in Zambia (opposite) and above is a trophy bull (No. 3 in the record book) bagged by the author after several unproductive kudu safaris.

The author's fine sable bull (below) is still No. 3 in Rowland Ward's *Records* and was taken near Kasempa on the Zambian-Angolan border.

shaped horns taping as much as 44 inches on the outside curve. A majority of the best heads have come from the Sahatu Mountains of northwest Gallaland, and the beast ranges to the east-northeast of Lake Zwai.

In the Sudan, grazing on waterlogged ground bordering the swamps along the White Nile and its tributaries, is another rare buck—Mrs. Gray's lechwe, a ski-footed 200-pound antelope with long coarse hair and a white saddle above its shoulders. It is a must for a hunter who wants top-drawer trophies—and not many men have bagged one.

Traveling west we come to the domain of the Barbary sheep, an elusive, tawny, and crafty rascal that inhabits the rugged red-rock mountains of Tibesti and Ennedi and most mountain ranges of north and north-eastern Africa from Morocco to Egypt. Nature has given this beast such wonderful camouflage that you can be looking right at one up on some ridge through powerful binoculars and unless he wiggles an ear you'll never see him. As in the case of the walia ibex, the problem is to shoot a ram where it's possible to retrieve him, not where he might drop a thousand feet or more to be smashed to bits.

In the heart of the Sahara lives one of the oddest of the antelopes, the addax. Nature gave him caribou feet to help negotiate the dunes, and spiral horns. Able to exist for long periods without water, the animal gets moisture from a tennis-ball sized melon.

South and east of the Sahara lies the Wadi Hachim, a dry riverbed of great width. On this vast stretch, flat as a parking lot for miles, can be found another wonderfully handsome antelope, the scimitar oryx, as great a test of a rifleman's skill as can be found. Traveling in herds of from a dozen to thirty or more animals, they are usually shot while they are at full gallop at distances varying from 300 to 500 yards, and when you bring down a record-class bull you'll think that you have earned him.

On the fringe of the Wadi Hachim and from Nigeria and Senegambia through Morocco to Kordofan is still another glamor candidate, this one a gazelle called dama and which the Arabs name Ariel. Its coat is basically white, looming up like alabaster in the sunlight, with rufous airbrush shading at the throat. Of all the African gazelles he is easily the handsomest.

In Oubangui-Chari, a day's ride out of Fort Archambault, one can hunt the savanna country for the grand-daddy of all the antelopes, the enormous Lord Derby's eland, a beast standing almost six feet high at the shoulder and about six times handsomer than a common East African eland. He has wonderful dark shading at the throat and a great bushy frontal tuft at the forehead, and his massive horns, sweeping back to a length of 40 inches or more, are superb. I rate a well-mounted head of this whopper as one of the most dramatic of all trophies to be taken anywhere.

The Holy Grail of all big-game hunters is, without argument, the bongo. This will-o'-the-wisp antelope, vaguely related to both kudu and eland, is found in a narrow diagonal forest belt stretching from Liberia on the West Coast, through Gabon and on across to Uganda and Kenya. Big, brave, and rather prone to attack when cornered, this is a truly magnificent animal and one of the world's top five trophies. So hard is he to come by that his name is mentioned with much respect by tyro and veteran alike, for many an expert hunter has spoored one up for days under arduous conditions and has actually been within ten yards of his quarry without getting a shot.

There are a few other trophy animals, somewhat less rare, which deserve to be mentioned in the glamor category. First of these, and no great beauty, is the hirola, or Hunter's hartebeeste, a rufous-colored buck with white facial chevron, which exists in only a single locality, a tiny patch of bush in Southern Somaliland on the north bank of the Tana River.

Another fine animal, hard to come by and almost extinct in Kenya, is the roan antelope, a big, powerful, and bad-tempered brute which, wounded, is more dangerous than a mad dog and a lot bigger. Some of the top heads come from West Africa and the Sudan, but I have found this species most numerous in what is now Zambia where horns of 30 inches can still be taken if one is able to visit the remote districts on the northwestern border.

Although by no means rare, I feel that the common waterbuck, *Kobus ellipsiprymnus*, also belongs in the glamor category not only due to my personal admiration but because he invariably reminded early British hunters, thanks to his stately dignity, of the stag of their homeland—and that is praise indeed. A 400-pound antelope with shaggy hair and superb horns, he exists, with a few gaps, from the Limpopo River in South Africa to the Webi Shebeli in Somaliland.

There is one other ibex in Africa very much worth going after if you don't mind blast-furnace heat, and that is the Nubian variety of the Red Sea Hills in the Sudan and Eritrea, Upper Egypt and Nubia. Not as large as the walia of Abyssinia, a good ram might tip the scales at 200 pounds but the horns might tape a shade longer, the record Nubian having a 2¼-inch edge on the record walia, although the circumference of the walia's horns at the base is much greater.

Still another exotic beast, not rare but extremely hard to find when you're looking for one, is the situtunga, a waterlogged ski-footed animal which—thanks to Turkish-slipper hooves—is unable to get around satisfactorily anywhere except in papyrus swamps, reed beds, and marshes. What makes him hard to find is his trick of submerging so that only his nostrils show above water. None of the glamor game trophies comes very easily—and that's why they're glamorous.

One of the rarest of African antelopes is the inyala, a husky member of the bushbuck family. The Zulus call him "The Shifty One," and like all bushbucks he can be dangerous on occasion.

OPPOSITE: The author and an Angoni guide with a handsome inyala bull taken at St. Lucia Bay where G. F. Angas discovered the beast in 1847.

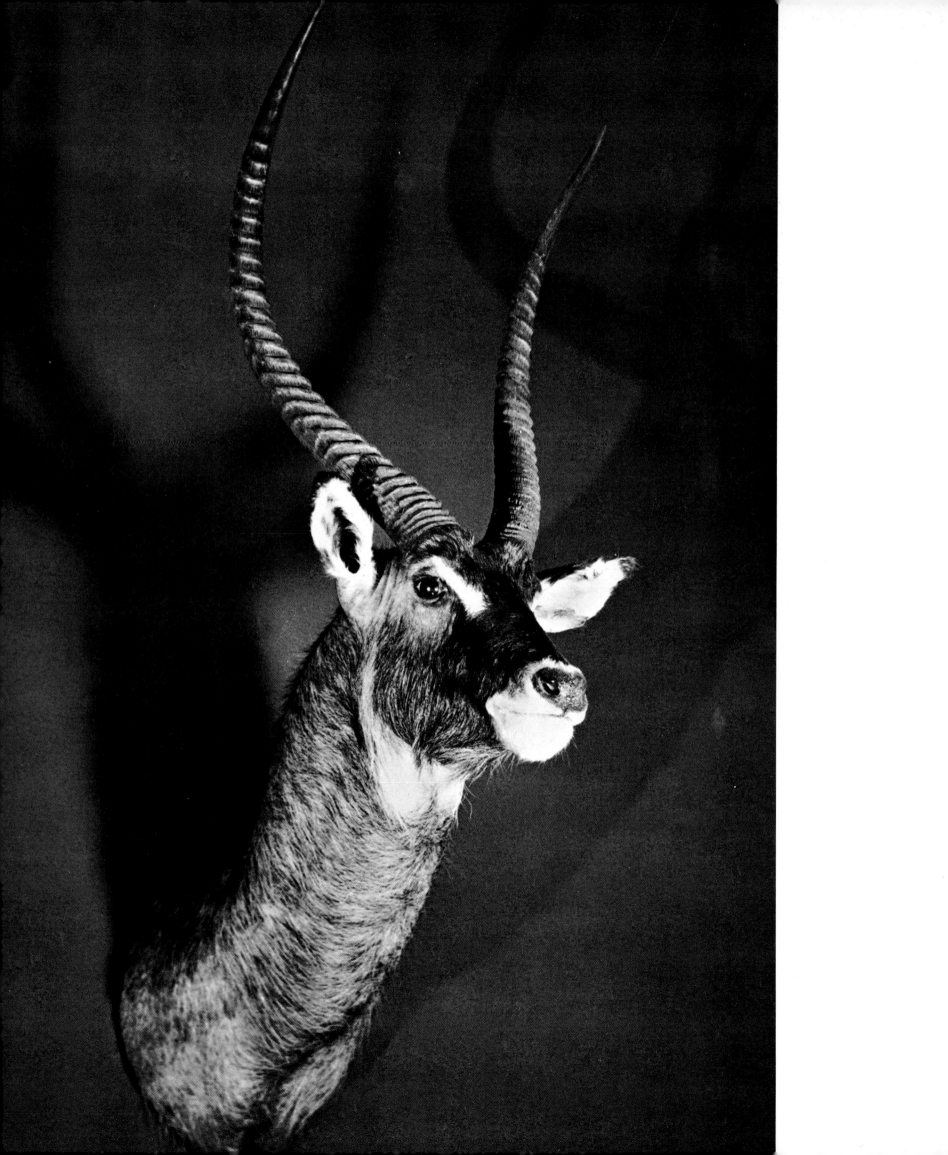

An old waterbuck bull in his prime carries himself with the majesty of a Scottish stag. Weighing 500 pounds, he has a heavy hairy coat. The remarkable head opposite is the author's No. 1 world record.

Lancer of the desert is the graceful and speedy scimitar oryx, called by the Arabs *Abu harab,* "father of spears." Racing across the great dry riverbeds flanking the Sahara at full gallop, he is an extremely difficult target.

The magnificent scimitar oryx bull (above) was a world record when it was bagged by the author on the Wadi Ha-chim in 1959. Three weeks later it was beaten and since then over a dozen better have won a spot in the *Records.*

ABOVE: Identical high-spine shots, the most merciful
type known, accounted for a fine double on beisa oryx
(*Oryx gazella beisa*) up on Kenya's northern frontier.
Properly executed, this shot drops a beast stone dead.

The fringe-eared oryx (*O. gazella callotis*) opposite is a
handsome antelope now becoming somewhat rare and
inhabits semi-desert country in Kenya and Tanzania.

The Barbary sheep (*Ammotragus lervia*) seen bawling his challenge, above, is known as aoudad to the crossword puzzle addict. Because of his hairy front legs, rather like fur chaps from old Western films, the French call him *Mouflon a Manchettes*—the sheep with the cuffs.

LEFT: Typical mouflon mountains in Ennedi on the edge of the Sahara near the Sudan border, looking like some parts of Arizona, an arid waste almost devoid of water.

Old Barbary rams are among the wariest of wild sheep and blend fantastically into the rocky terrain. They become vulnerable when they climb down the near-vertical cliffsides to drink at a *guelta*, a waterhole.

The author's giant sable (below) is No. 12 in Rowland Ward's *Records*. Studying the head is Prince Alexander Auersperg, whose ancestor's world record 1-day chamois bag still stands.

THE GIANT SABLE ANTELOPE

Rarest and most fabulous of African glamor game is *Hippotragus niger variani*, the giant sable antelope. This husky, wary, and wonderfully handsome buck roams a patch of bush roughly thirty miles wide in Angola. His habitat is a triangle of land heavily pockmarked with salt pans and bracketed between two swift-flowing rivers, the Luando and the Quanza. Another river, the Luaco, completes the water barrier guarding his domain.

The Portuguese of Angola call this animal *Palanca preta*, and to the local Luimbe tribesmen he is known as *sumba kaloko*. What makes him one of the greatest of trophies are his horns, massive annulated weapons which sweep in mighty arcs back toward his rump. The coat on a bull in his prime might range in color from chocolate brown to almost coal black, and the mask is extremely decorative.

Prior to 1913 a single outsize horn in the Natural History Museum in Florence had excited the curiosity of many a sportsman, including Frederick Selous. "I measured this phenomenal horn," he wrote, "and I am sure that there is no mistake about its length of 61 inches, though where it came from nobody knows."

The mystery was solved in 1913 by H. F. Varian, an engineer for the Benguela Railway, who sent back to London the skin, cape, and horns of an Angolan sable which the Zoological Society hailed as a new and superior species officially classified as *variani*, a trophy which fewer than 50 hunters have bagged.

George Parker, noted Arizona big-game hunter, with his fine giant sable, No. 26 in the *Records,* shot on a special Museum Permit in 1954. Today this superb beast is strictly protected.

The savanna country of the Central African Republic is the home of the Lord Derby's eland *(Taurotragus derbianus)*. Hunting is very difficult due to a carpet of dry leaves, like giant cornflakes, and extreme heat. Favorite food of the giant is eland bush *(Isoberlinia doka)* in photo above.

A powerful porter is needed to carry the head of a giant Lord Derby's eland back to base camp due to the fact that skull and horns often weigh 150 pounds and the temperature might hit 120 degrees.

Somali trackers bring in a gerenuk, the giraffe-necked gazelle of East Africa, Abyssinia, and Somaliland. Contrary to the white hunter's orders, they have cut the throat in the Mohammedan *halal*.

We flew Explorers Club Flag No. 176 at camp in Wadi Hachim. Below, a rare record-book Hunter's hartebeeste in N. Kenya.

Dingalo, the author's Barotse tracker, with a fine gemsbok bull (No. 7 in Rowland Ward *Records*) from the Kalahari Desert. This is the biggest of the four African oryx species.

SAFARI CARS

The oldtime foot safari (above) was romantic but grueling, since tons of food and equipment had to be toted on the heads of porters.

IN the early days of safari the hunter went on foot, accompanied by at least a hundred porters carrying packs weighing a maximum of 60 pounds on their heads. By forty years ago, in the heyday of Martin and Osa Johnson, flimsy touring cars were being used with a somewhat limited success, and by the late thirties a practical and tough safari vehicle had evolved using a husky ton-and-a-half International truck to which a fine teak body had been fitted by Hindu craftsmen in Nairobi. It had no doors, so one could instantly dismount for a stalk when game was sighted, and behind the front seat was a fine gunrack with quick-detachable clamps holding one's entire battery of weapons—small-bore, big-bore, express, and shotgun. It also had, after World War II, a tank-com-

mander's hatch in the top from which one could take excellent pictures from a high and safe vantage point. It had an instant success, was used over a span of years, and you probably saw such safari cars in films like *The Macomber Affair* and *The Snows of Kilimanjaro.*

Since then there have been vogues for Power Wagons, Jeeps, the rugged British Land Rover (now leading in popularity), and even a $35,000 German *Unimoc.*

Clients get quite attached to these modern hunting cars which, with special gears and tough tires, make their own roads and have been able to penetrate distant areas and come back with world's record heads. Their counterparts can now be seen on Texas ranches.

ABOVE: The classic International Safari Car   BELOW: The German *Unimoc*

Jumping-off point for the Sahara is the red mud fort at
Oum Chalouba where Gourane trackers (in foreground) are
hired to guide the hunter across the endless wastes of
the Wadi Hachim, a great dry river bed flat as pavement.

In the days before Independence, the French Colonial Army lived a true *Beau Geste* existence at forts dotted throughout the Sahara. At the oasis of Fada, Captain Lambotte is preparing to mount his racing camel for the desert patrol.

THE BONGO

Holy Grail of the big-game hunter in Africa is the bongo (*Boocercus eurycerus*), one of the top ten trophies in the world. A big bull will weigh in at 500 pounds and is ultra-wary and truculent, being prone to charge if cornered. A forest-dweller, he is found in a narrow belt of dense forest which extends from Kenya in the east through the Congo and across to Sierra Leone.

This gives the hunter two choices of terrain as a locale for his quest. He can hunt Kenya and its Aberdares where he will make daily climbs through thick forests of podo and olive and cedar, tripping over unseen lianas, battling the stinging nettles, and acquiring tomato-red eyes from the powder falling like rain in the bamboo thickets. He will climb and climb and climb, playing tag with crusty Cape buffalo, leopard, and giant forest hog, clear to the moorlands at the top, often wreathed in mist. He will wait interminable hours in a machan near a salt lick, he will hunt each stream and ravine, and in all probability by two weeks later will never have had a shot.

The other choice is grimmer—the forest and swamp wilderness of the Moyen Congo and neighboring lands. Here one generally slogs, waist deep, through the awful stinking swamps, gasping in the 135-degree heat and oppressive humidity, fighting off leeches in the water and fire-ants when crossing an occasional bit of dry land, using shy Babinga pygmies as trackers. The foliage is so dense that the chances are rather good that if you get a shot at all it will be at a 3-inch patch of reddish-brown hide—if you're naturally lucky. You will have earned your trophy.

Slogging through the miasmic swamps of the Moyen Congo, Babinga pygmies track the bongo like a pack of beagles, occasionally stopping (left) to sniff for scent. In the stinking yellow swamps, sweltering from the incredible heat and humidity, one is constantly scraping off leeches in the water and fire ants on the few strips of dry land you cross. Bongo (right) was bagged for a museum.

Two rare trophies are the dama gazelle, or Ariel (above) found on the fringe of the Sahara, and the addax (at left, with veteran hunter-writer Frank Delano) which lives in the desert dunes and drinks no water, existing on small melons.

OPPOSITE: A Sara-Kaba girl in a small village in Oubangui-Chari holds the skull and horns of the author's No. 1 world's record western roan.

HUNTING WITH A CAMERA

SIXTY years ago A. Radclyffe Dugmore used a reflex camera, big as a breadbox and weighing 17 pounds, to snap a superlative action photograph of a rhinoceros in full charge. This, mind you, on glass plates with an emulsion pitifully slow by today's standards and far too fragile to stand much bouncing around in the bushveldt.

Today most photographers of wild animals carry the compact 35 mm. cameras with fast lenses and telephoto lenses of various lengths, the most popular being the 135 mm. I used this lens on the Contax for many years, then switched to the 180 mm. Sonnar f2.8 on the same camera, using it with a neck harness. Later when the vogue for through-the-lens reflex type cameras came along I changed to the Contarex using both 55 mm. and 135 mm. lenses extensively. The one I use most today, I find, is the Nikon F with motor drive film transport and backed by the fine 200 mm. lens.

Assuming that you have accumulated the photographic equipment in which you feel confidence, the next most important ingredient for getting admirable animal photographs is patience. Extreme telephoto lenses such as 500 mm. and 1000 mm. lack the crisp definition of those of fewer diameters, and therefore what you must learn is how to stalk, moving one cautious step at a time when a beast drops its head to feed or is looking the opposite way. You must watch the wind every second so that you can remain downwind from your target, and in Africa I used to tote along a small burlap sack, no bigger than a pack of cigarettes, full of wood ash. Shaking out this fine powder gave me a positive reading of the wind.

No sudden motion should ever be made, and it is of course highly desirable that your safari clothing be a neutral shade which blends into the terrain where you are working, since a white shirt will scare all game into the next county. While the average photographer works with the sun behind him, a specialist will move carefully to a spot where he can put modeling quality into his lighting.

To get exciting pictures it is often necessary to take chances, and one can get into plenty of trouble in the process. In my many attempts to make colorful close-up pictures of angry elephants, Cape buffaloes, rhinos, and lions I have had some very narrow squeaks indeed—but I usually got the picture. Looking back on it in retrospect, it was a whale of a lot of fun.

If you remain downwind and freeze when an animal looks your way, it is possible to approach even a hulking Cape buffalo bull.

ASIA

The cheetah, (above) trained by Maharajahs to catch and kill the fleet blackbuck, now is extinct in India. The Manchurian tiger, (opposite) much bigger and heavier than the Bengal type, is a rare and magnificent cat.

THOSE who hunt great game in Asia never forget the experience. Years later, when they think of it in retrospect, a magic carpet of exotic names flashes by on the screen of memory—names like Naini Tal and Nagpur, Kumaon, Hyderabad, Bandipur, Bharatpur, Gilgit, and Baltit. These are followed in close succession by mental pictures of jheel and jungle and kadir, of craggy peaks towering into fleecy clouds—Tien Shan, the Hindu Kush, Karakoram, the fabled Pamirs and the rocky majesty of the forbidding Khyber Pass.

When one heads toward the Far East, rifle in hand, India always beckons first, for it is the gateway to the vast wild stretches of Asia which lie beyond. It is impossible to go on shikar in India without feeling the weight of the countless centuries of civilization this hoary land has known. Compared to some upper-bracket Indian nobility, the celebrated ancient kings of England were parvenus, the crowned heads of Europe mere Johnny-come-latelies. His Highness the Maharajah of Udaipur, a man of immense dignity, could claim membership in the oldest family known on earth, his ancestry traceable back through 140 generations, to a time before Agamemnon and the Trojan Wars. There are still Indian princes who on state occasions ride to the ceremonies in silver palanquins, studded with rubies, emeralds and diamonds, which would make the Coronation Coach of the Hapsburgs look like a Model-T Ford.

Hunting in India is entirely different from any encountered elsewhere—very exotic and effortless, or extremely difficult and frustrating, depending on *who* you are and where you are.

In the department of sheer swank there is nothing to match the elegance of hunting as guest of a ranking Maharajah. You might find yourself living in a pink palace in a bedroom big enough to house a troop of Bengal Lancers, with hot and cold running servants to cater to your slightest whim, and formal dinners of roast peacock soaked in olive oil, tenderized with papaya juice and somewhat spicy to Western tastes.

To get to a tiger-beat your transportation would in all probability be a Rolls-Royce (one potentate used to keep a dozen just for hunting parties) and you'd end up, if at Mysore, in a super-deluxe *machan* up in a tree, with two rows of seats like an opera box. Or you may be conveyed to the teak tiger forest on the top deck of a royal pad elephant painted in psychedelic designs and guaranteed to pitch and toss like a shrimp boat in a hurricane. When the drums say a tiger is coming you'd better be ready to shoot fast.

In India, you see, there is sometimes a small fly in the ointment and in this case it's the simple fact that almost every Maharajah is trying for a score on tiger a bit better than his nearest rival's. Consequently his trigger finger is itchy and heaven help your high hopes if Mr. Stripes passes closer to his *machan*.

After all, rank has its privileges and if you're going to be a sybarite shikari you can't have everything.

The few Maharajahs who run commercial shikars for a hand-picked clientele do everything in their power to try to get their guests an opportunity to shoot a tiger.

If you're the average sportsman, the chances are that you'll never see a Maharajah. You'll make your booking through a Shikar Agency, probably in Nagpur, where you'll be outfitted, and you will motor cross-country a couple of hundred miles to reach your allotted tiger blocks, cursing all bullock carts as you run an obstacle course the entire distance. You won't go by Rolls-Royce but you might as well have, because the second-hand Chevrolet Impala in which you travel has set your outfitter back a cool $14,000 due to import restrictions. As a client you'll live in a comfortable adobe bungalow with tiled roof, courtesy of

The Mohammedan gunbearer and headman from a village called Kiror might have stepped right out of the pages of *Lives of a Bengal Lancer*.

The Indian bear, Baloo, is feared more by the primitive villagers than is the mighty tiger. He is bad-tempered and has very poor eyesight.

the Forestry Department, and if it's hot weather (in late April and May it's hotter than a pan-fried pork chop) you'll inherit a relay of local Baigas or Gonds outside your door at night to pull the rope which activates the *punkah* over your bed, a primitive form of air conditioning. To keep you comfortable there will be a staff of ten besides your hunter: waiter, valet, cook, skinner, waterboy, and their subordinates.

You'll sleep well on an air mattress atop a *charpoy*, and the food will be generally good. Instead of roast peacock, because the peacock is now the national bird of India and strictly protected, you'll have chicken Tandoori, red as a boiled lobster. Not every cook in India can handle occidental recipes with complete success, but they try hard. In a country where cows are sacred you are not likely to find much roast beef listed on the menu.

If and when you do find a tiger—and they've been iffy for a long time—you'll be in the same spot as the bloke who is guest of a Maharajah, only in your case it's the professional hunter whom you'll have to beat to the draw. All too many clients, incredible as it may seem, have arrived in India to slay a tiger without ever having killed even a rabbit, and battle-scarred shikaris are getting understandably jumpy.

And some of them are dead.

Tiger hunting is not Ping-Pong, and if you're a green-as-grass tyro you'd *better* permit your shikari to shoot at the same time. A big male tiger can kill an ox with one clout of a paw that is only slightly smaller than a catcher's mitt. Wounded, he will fight until his last gasp, and in full angry charge is one of the most frightening sights in the world, a black-striped orange bundle of catapulting muscle and murder. An elastic ligament in his windpipe, instead of bone, allows a great extension of the larynx and results in a roar which at close range is absolutely paralyzing in intensity. If there's one thing I can do without nicely it's a 500-pound tiger, wounded but not incapacitated, in dense jungle.

If you are a crack rifle shot with many major trophies to your credit on other hunts, you can safely explain to your shikari that you do not wish collaboration except in an emergency.

And don't fumble the shot.

If you succeed in bagging a big tiger, you'll find that you treasure his magnificent pelt over and above most other prizes of the chase.

But India has another great trophy beast to titillate a head-hunter, the gaur or Indian bison, known as *seladang* in Malaysia, largest of all wild oxen of our globe. Bigger in body than a Kenai moose, an old bull stands almost six foot six at the shoulder and takes more killing than an African Cape buffalo. The gaur is hunted on special license only and at times is placed under full protection.

This huge beast is spoored up in bamboo thickets, no easy task due to his high-powered ears and keen nose. He is also taken in the early morning when he leaves the forest to graze, and late in the afternoon when he repairs to a favorite waterhole. In some districts he is taken more easily by shooting from a howdah atop an elephant, a method usually afforded visiting royalty. Since the gaur, cornered, can be an extremely dangerous animal, the elephant is a form of life insurance.

Another big brute is the Indian buffalo, with superb horns which might tape better than five feet from tip to tip and up to 77 inches on the outside curve. His days are numbered, however, and already he has become extinct in Bihar and Bengal. A special license to hunt him is necessary in many areas, and while he is rarely dangerous when in a herd, a solitary bull is likely to charge and is capable of killing a man without working up a sweat.

There is also the panther, a cat virtually identical to the African leopard except that as an average it runs smaller in size. Most panthers are shot over a bait in the late afternoon or night, a close range shot that presents few problems. Others are bagged at night when encountered while cruising in a jeep, targets of opportunity which require a carefully aimed shot to avoid having to plunge into black jungle with a flashlight to locate a wounded and highly dangerous beast.

A bad actor in the middleweight class is the wild boar, a sharp-tusked brute that might tip the scales at 360 pounds and has a temper like a tarantula. When angry, which is often, he will take on any opponent and give most of them a bad time, being husky enough to overturn a horse and rider. If you happen to meet a big boar at close range while on foot, better make sure that you drop him stone dead with the first bullet or he's liable to slash you open like a burglar looking for money in a mattress.

India also has bears.

The Himalayan black bear, a brawny beast with a big white V on his chest like a varsity sweater, is found in the forests of northern India and also in Kashmir. The sloth bear, found in Central India, has a heavy snout, flabby lips like a camel, walks like a drunken sailor, and possesses the disposition of a dragon. Most villagers fear him more than they do the tiger and for good reason, many having had their faces lacerated to hamburger by this ugly devil. As a rule the sloth bear will avoid man wherever possible, but his eyesight is poor and if surprised at close range he will usually attack and is a vicious, dirty fighter in a clinch.

Farther to the northeast is the domain of the Tibetan blue bear, a rare animal whose cured pelt is occasionally palmed off to chumps as the skin of the yeti, the Abominable Snowman.

India is also blessed with a profusion of deer, the three major species being the sambar, the barasingha or swamp deer, and the chital or axis deer.

The barasingha, a 400-pound beast with antlers up to 41 inches on the outside curve, is on the road to extinction and is now protected. He has a cousin to the north, the hangul, or Kashmir barasingha, which is one of the great trophies of the world. Living in the forests on the northern slopes of the Vale of Kashmir, at altitudes of 12,000 feet in the summer, this great deer has magnificent antlers taping up to 50 inches on the outside curve. Turkestan has a similar trophy, the Yarkand stag, which is 50 pounds lighter, and although the horns are somewhat shorter they are much thicker, like a good Carpathian stag.

The sambar is a big deer of 600 pounds with coarse shaggy hair, a large and bushy tail, and antlers which terminate in a fork, making them less impressive than other large deer of the world. It is not easy to find a sambar stag with a really good head these days, and a poor one is not a trophy of which one would be overly proud.

The chital, on the other hand, is one of the handsomest deer to be found and is reasonably abundant. He has a spotted coat like the European fallow deer; his antlers are beautifully shaped and sweep back to a length of up to 40 inches on the outside curve, remarkable on a cervine animal in the 200-pound class.

Two other medium-sized species are the hog deer and the antler-browed deer of Manipur. Then there is the small barking deer, or muntjac, which stands 21 inches at the shoulder and weighs an average of 35 pounds. His antlers are generally five to six inches in length, consisting of a stunted brow tine and an unbranched beam supported on long skin-covered pedicles. Even smaller is the tiny mouse deer, a nocturnal creature with an inordinately long body in proportion to its height, hoofs so small as to seem unlikely, and a head which reminds me of an oversize guinea pig. Tiny as is the Indian species, my old friend Jimmy Clark, on an expedition of the American Museum of Natural History, shot one in Indo-China which was only 8 inches in height at the shoulder and weighed 4 pounds.

There are scores of other Asian trophies. Blackbuck, a distant relative of the African springbok and gerenuk, is a small antelope weighing only 85 pounds with handsome spiral horns, the best specimens taping just under 30 inches. Currently this species is protected.

Up on the India-Burma border lives the queer takin, largest of the goat-antelopes, an awkward animal ten hands in height and weighing up to 500 pounds, which is a relative of the musk-ox. This border species is grayish-brown in color but he has a cousin in Shensi Province in China which has orange-yellow hair and is believed to be the great "ram with the golden fleece" sought by Jason in the old Greek legends. In that ban-

dit-ridden country, where he is called *yeh-niu* (wild cow) he inhabits bamboo jungles at an altitude of at least 10,000 feet. He is not easy to stalk.

For those who like to climb, the upper slopes of the Himalayas offer some rare and wary special trophies. There are fine wild sheep: shapo or urial, and bharal (blue sheep). There are wild goats: ibex, markhor, and tahr, the latter a beardless quadruped with a ruff to fluff in courting season so that he looks a bit like he's wearing a fur cape. Then for good measure there are two other goat-antelopes, the serow and goral, and their natural enemy—the snow leopard, a real prize.

India also has the nilgai, or blue bull, a hulking antelope with big feet, short horns and front legs longer than the hind ones. Serious shikaris consider him hardly worth the effort. Of more interest is the chousingha, or four-horned antelope, rufous brown in coloration and weighing about 40 pounds.

There are three superb trophies found elsewhere in Asia but they are unfortunately out-of-bounds behind the Iron Curtain, and the risks involved, even if permission could be granted, would be very grim indeed. Perhaps greatest of them all is the magnificent Manchurian tiger, a huge and regal beast with luxuriantly heavy fur and a massive body, much bigger and more powerful than the Indian species. Very few hunters have been fortunate enough to bag this top prize.

A lot of serious sportsmen claim that the king of them all is the *Ovis poli* of the Pamir plateau, the great wild sheep with massive corkscrew horns which was first described by its discoverer, Marco Polo, upon his return from the court of Kublai Khan back in the latter part of the 12th Century.

Other enthusiasts give the palm to the fine ibex of the Tien Shan, a bearded beast of better than 200 pounds whose massive annulated horns sweep back in great arcs to form one of the most dramatic trophies.

Elsewhere in that corner of the globe the big-game picture is spotty. In Japan the Ainu still kill—and worship—the brown bear. Australia was completely shortchanged in the big-game department but well stocked with large crocodiles and snakes. New Zealand is a Shanghri-La bristling with big game today, but all of the animals have been imported—red and fallow deer and chamois from Europe; sambar, axis, and Japanese deer and tahr from Asia; and moose, wapiti, and whitetail deer from North America. All have done well and in some cases have grown better horns than specimens in their homeland. Commercial meat hunting has thinned them in recent years.

If a man were to start hunting at the age of seven and lived to be a hundred and fifty, he might possibly have time to hunt half of the magnificent beasts which roam the jungles, mountains, and steppes of the vast Asian hunting terrain.

The axis deer, or chital, has few rivals when it comes to beauty of form and color. Once numerous, its tribe has been decimated by poachers.

The hog deer or para (*Axis porcinus*), a short-legged deer of 100 pounds weight, inhabits the Indus Valley to Assam, Tenasserim, Burma, Siam.

A tiger is full grown at two years and lethal from the age of six months. His sense of smell is only fair but his eyes are very sharp, and shikaris swear that he can recognize colors distinctly on the blackest of nights.

OPPOSITE: This big tiger has returned to finish a kill, in this case a half-grown buffalo, tame, called a *boda.*

THE TIGER

Philadelphia's David Hasinger (above) bagged this enormous tiger, high in the record book, while out on shikar in Northern India in 1967.

ABOVE the Ganges, on top of a hill at Siligarhi, is a domed grave—the tomb of a Moslem saint—and both Moslems and Hindus used to tell of a huge tiger with fiercely glowing eyes which came every night to pay its respects and stand vigil like some grim sentinel until dawn's early light. Many a sacred tomb in Asia has been looted by grave-robbers at one time or other, but not *that* one.

Such an aura of magic, mystery, and mayhem surrounds the Indian tiger that many aboriginal tribes—Baigas, Bhils, and Gonds—regard him with a superstitious awe and worship him in both actual and mythical form, offering little presents to him on red-painted rocks at the foot of a sacred fig tree.

For the same reason that American Indians devoured the heart of the grizzly bear, to gain courage, so do these primitive folk eat the flesh of the tiger. If you don't keep an eye on them they will also try to singe the whiskers of your trophy to prevent it from returning to life as a were-tiger, a *tuindak*. To them he is Sher Khan, incarnation of an imperishable and potent god, and if there are those among them who refuse to aid a shikari in spooring up this Lord of the Stripes, who can blame them? Certainly not those of us who will not walk under a ladder or sit thirteen at table.

The Bengal tiger is a noble beast, a gentleman to the core and one of the handsomest trophies that any big-game hunter can ever hope to bag. Unfortunately he has been stigmatized, unjustly, as bloodthirsty and cruel when in fact he is no more so than the common house cat when you allow for the proportionate increase in size. A normal tiger, unmolested by man, will mind his own business just so long as you mind yours. Very recently while on shikar in Madhya Pradesh I was trying to get a shot at a great brute of a tiger only slightly smaller than a polo pony, the Devil Tiger of Kiror. An exceptionally crafty beast, he would never come back directly to his kill on the next evening, instead would sneak up after midnight, when you were already jittery after seven long hours of patient sitting, and calmly take a stand right under the *machan* to park for a solid hour in a calculated war of nerves. In ten grueling days and nights of nonstop hunting, with the temperature standing at 120 degrees, I cursed him often but never laid eyes on the old rascal.

Yet one morning our water carrier, a Gond woman

of dark complexion, came screaming into the compound as white as a marshmallow. Just as she started across a road in the forest above the spring, the enormous tiger had emerged from the opposite side, also crossing. They passed within ten feet of each other, the tiger merely regarding the woman in curiosity, the woman herself in a complete state of shock. Yet this same animal had been known to kill a big cow with one swat, pick it up by the nape of the neck, and hurl it twenty feet with a toss of his head.

Needless to say, not all tigers can be written off as nondangerous. A wounded one is a holy terror, as dangerous to face as an African elephant on the prod. A female with cubs can be very dangerous indeed—but so can a domestic sow with farrow.

A man-eater is something else again.

A man-eater may have become one for a variety of reasons. Most commonly he is an old tiger too slow and weak to catch game or kill a cow by himself and as a result turns to the human race. Other man-eaters are those wounded at some earlier date that have escaped to wage war on their two-legged persecutors. Some of the others got a taste for human flesh from corpses left in the wake of famine or epidemic. At any rate, once a tiger has made a meal of a human, he usually puts it as No. 1 on his menu from then on. There have been some truly terrible man-eaters in India, perhaps the worst being a family of them at Bhiwapur, a long time ago, which killed and ate 400 people before the rest of the inhabitants finally fled.

Tigers have rarely been so plentiful that a shikari could be certain of bagging one. Way back in 1904 a book by Aflalo had this to say: "The keenest and best shot in the world, without influence or introductions to those who know the game, might spend a dozen years hunting in India without getting a shot at a tiger."

There are three basic methods of bagging a tiger, commonest involving sitting up in a *machan* from late afternoon until dawn over a *boda*, a 2-year-old buffalo either alive or killed by the tiger the previous night. In the second method the hunter is perched in a *machan* as beaters try to drive a localized animal in the direction of the gun. With the third method elephants are used as beaters, the shot being taken from the comparative security of a mattress strapped to a pad elephant or in some cases from a howdah.

Zoologists believe that the tiger entered India from Northern Asia after the last Ice Age, through China and past the eastern end of the Himalayas. Tigers are solitary and visit a regular series of locales when hunting food. Many shikaris say that this beast kills only once in ten days.

"Most beautiful deer in the world" is what they call the axis deer, or chital, (*Cervus axis*) whose white-spotted hide remains that way at all seasons and at all stages. These Asiatic deer do not separate, stags, hinds, and fawns clanning up together.

Photograph by Mary Hurn

His Highness the Maharajah of Cooch-Behar (in levis and low-crowned Spanish hat), a great big-game hunter himself as was his father before him, with two of his pad elephants, a huge male tiger, and American friends just finishing their shikar.

John B. LaGarde, noted big-game hunter of Piedmont, Alabama, with a fine specimen of Asiatic ibex (above) and at left with the twisty-horned markhor (*Capra falconeri*) which roams the Himalayas from Kashmir to the Hindu Kush.

OPPOSITE: H.I.H. Prince Abdorezza of Iran with a great Pasang or wild goat (*Capra hircus aegagrus*) of Asia Minor and Persia, the progenitor of the European tame goat.

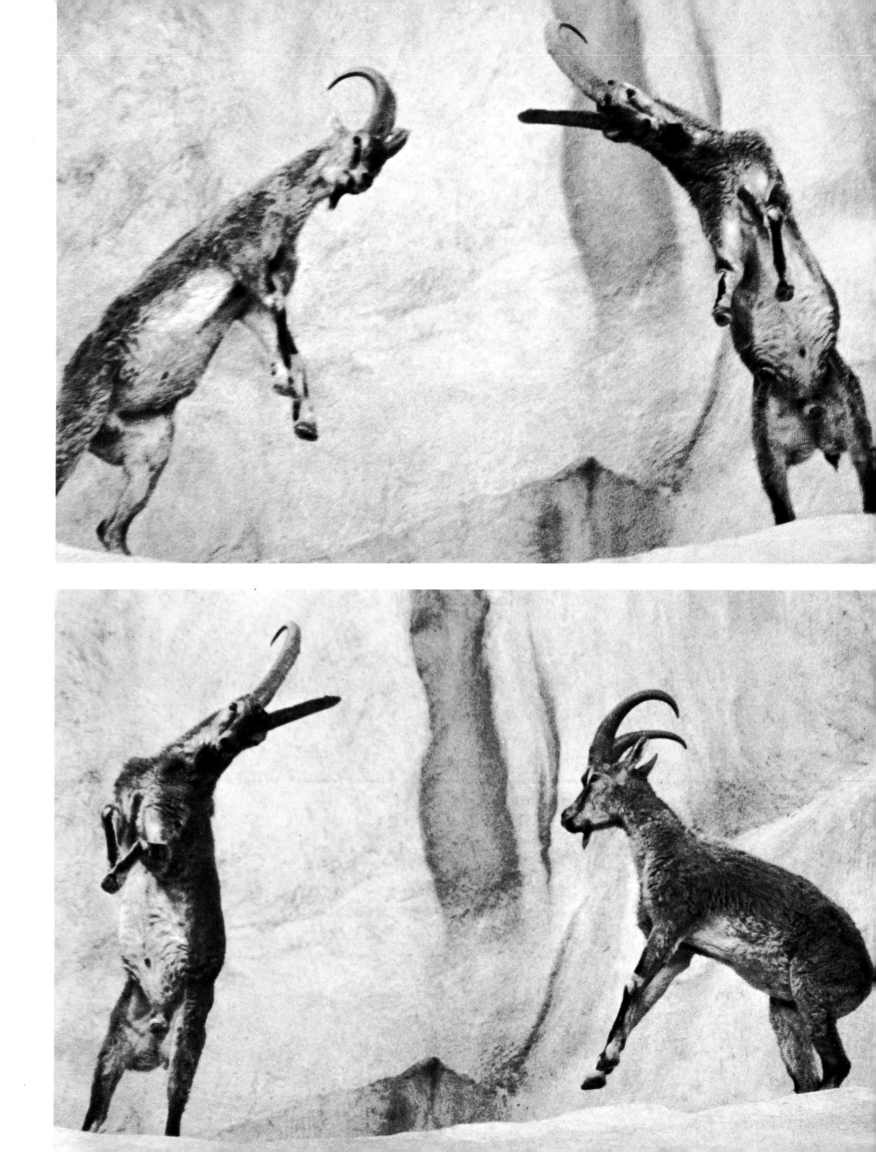

The takin (*Budorcas taxicolor*), called by the Chinese *yeh-niu* (wild cow) is a rare goat-antelope found in Bhutan, Tibet, and northern Assam. The Chinese animal is yellow, lives in bamboo jungles at 10,000 feet in the Tsing-ling Mts. of Shensi Province and is thought to be Jason's "ram with the Golden Fleece."

To bag this superb 400-pound Mongolian argali (*Ovis ammon*) California's ace big-game hunter Elgin Gates traveled 15,000 miles via Ulan Bator and the Gobi Desert to the High Altai.

THE MARCO POLO SHEEP

"SUICIDE Sheep" is the name they ought to give the *Ovis poli*, the great wild sheep of the Pamir plateau, for the pursuit of him is fraught with many perils. Today, due to the Iron Curtain, he can be hunted only in one place, the tiny principality of Hunza which lies where the Hindu Kush and Karakoram meet, and then only if you have a personal invitation from the Mir, His Highness Mohammed Jamal Khan, special permission from the President of Pakistan, plus a clearance from the political agent at Gilgit. This allows you to attempt to reach Hunza on horseback over a treacherous mountain trail scarcely two feet wide with a dropoff of 3,000 feet straight down into the rapids of the raging Hunza River. If you arrive in one piece, you still have no guarantee that you will see one of the great rams, for only occasionally do they drift over from Red China into the valleys of Shimshal and Khunjerab.

Only a man in superb physical condition, with some mountain climbing experience, could hope to survive a grueling hunt such as this, and it is one of the reasons why this handsome trophy is prized more than any other to be found in the world. There is danger of high altitude diseases such as pulmonary edema, pneumonia, frostbite and, even worse, heart attack, in the assault of almost vertical slopes. On top of that there is the constant threat of avalanches and of the dread "white-out" when the whole world disappears behind an opaque curtain of swirling snow. It is small wonder that those hardy few who have survived such a hunt and bagged the mighty Marco Polo sheep are the envy of all other big-game hunters. When Elgin Gates went after this trophy, in the fall of 1959, he had to cross a ridge on Chapchingal at 20,800 feet with the thermometer at 14 below zero, and it is a miracle that he came back alive.

The *Ovis poli* is a husky beast, standing 50 inches at the shoulder and weighing up to an estimated 450 pounds, and there are probably not more than a dozen sportsmen alive today who can claim his scalp.

Neighbors in the High Himalayas are these three animals, the snow leopard *(Felis uncia)* at left, the Asiatic ibex, or sakin (above), and the tahr *(Hemitragus jehamicus)* at right, who fluffs out his ruff when courting or if angry.

ROYAL BENGALS

THE tiger, noblest of Indian game, has been hunted by royalty of one stripe or another since the beginning of time. There was scarcely a single Moghul Emperor who wouldn't rather hunt tiger than eat, starting with the founder, Babar, who killed the cat with bow and arrow in the 16th Century. Over 125 years before that his ancestor, the great Tamerlane himself, also hunted the striped terror with considerable zest. In the 18th Century the Nawab Vizir of Oudh organized his tiger hunts like a military campaign, taking into the field with him 10,000 cavalry, 10,000 foot soldiers, 800 elephants, and a host of retainers. This was still done, on a smaller scale, when visiting royalty came to India in the early part of this century. When, in 1911, His Majesty King George V hunted in Nepal, he and his party killed 39 tigers in ten days, a phenomenal bag. The best single day's bag for the royal party was seven tigers, a near-record only equaled by the kill of the Maharajah of Cooch-Behar in 1907 and exceeded only once when Sir Russell Baker's party managed to bag eight tigers in 1897.

British military personnel stationed in India during the 19th Century took to tiger hunting with zest and produced many noted tiger slayers, the pluckiest being Sir James Outram, called the "Bayard of India," whose feat of successfully spearing a tiger has never been duplicated. HRH The Prince of Wales, later King Edward VII, hunted the tiger with great gusto, and within the past decade Her Majesty the Queen accompanied HRH The Duke of Edinburgh on his shikar as guest of a famed Indian sportsman, H.H. The Maharajah of Jaipur.

Photo courtesy C. Lancaster & Co. (Ltd.)

His Majesty, King George V, (above center) surveys a fine day's bag of tiger in Nepal in 1911. At left he is seen shooting from the royal howdah during his epic ten-day shikar.

Photo by Ernest Brooks

THE GAUR

ONE of the more exciting big-game animals of Asia is the gaur, or Indian bison (*Bibos gaurus*), known as *seladang* in Malaysia, greatest of all the wild oxen of the world. Standing six feet six at the shoulder and weighing up to 2,700 pounds, this big beast has a peculiar ridge, running parallel to the spine, from the withers to the middle of the back and terminating in quite an abrupt step. For all his bulk he has neat white stockings on delicate legs and a cap of beige hair on his concave forehead. Shy, he shelters in the bamboo thickets and comes to water in the very late afternoon or during the night.

The gaur has poor eyesight but a sharp nose and has enormous vitality, being harder to knock down with a single shot than the African Cape buffalo. Not basically aggressive as a species, old bull gaurs often become cranky and will charge savagely if cornered, somewhat paradoxical in an animal which, in mating season, whistles like a bird. His only enemies are tigers and men and it takes two tigers to bring one down.

The Indian elephant *(Elephas maximus)* is much smaller than the African species and a really big tusk on a bull today might not weigh over 60 pounds. Rogues and bulls in *musth* are dangerous but this is not a true hunting trophy.

A mature gaur in his prime, such as the 2300-pound bull opposite, is a top trophy found in few game bags. This prize fell to my rifle after hard hunting and manifold disappointments in the teak forests of India's Raipur blocks.

The chital, or axis deer, opposite, attain a weight of 200 pounds and dread the wild dog more than the tiger. The photograph at left demonstrates their use of natural camouflage.

The muntjac, or barking deer (*Muntiacus muntjac*), stands barely 21 inches at the shoulder, weighs roughly 35 pounds, is common in India.

The nilgai, or blue bull of India *(Boselaphus tragocamelus)*
is an ungainly heavyweight of the antelope family. Because
the *gai* of the name means cow, this animal is regarded as
sacred by the Hindus. Few sportsmen molest this odd beast.

122

Typical of the veteran shikaris of India is Krishna Sharma (right) who for twenty years has ably guided clients on big-game shikars, although he originally studied for the law. He holds the rare mouse-deer, or chevrotain.

THE SHIKARI

THE shikari, the professional hunter of India, has many different problems than has the white hunter of Africa, the *jaeger* of Europe, or the registered guide of North America.

The tiger is his specialty and he must know where to go and how best to bring about a confrontation between his client and the big striped cat which rates as one of the greatest and handsomest sporting trophies in the world.

Because the usual method of getting a shot at this animal requires an all-night vigil in a *machan* constructed near the bait, many shikaris develop night-vision almost as good as that of their prey. A shikari must know his terrain thoroughly in order to run a tiger beat in daylight, and possess the requisite courage and marksmanship to enable him to lead his client to the tiger if it has been only wounded. He must also know how to utilize a herd of tame buffalo to spoor up such a wounded animal. His reputation for bravery will have much to do with his success in rounding up the natives, Gonds and Baigas, who make up his line of beaters.

A shikari must also be ready to take his client in pursuit of other dangerous game such as buffalo, a really mean brute, and gaur, a great wild ox which can be very aggressive on occasion. To accommodate a customer who seeks the fabulous wild sheep and goat-antelopes of the high Himalayas, he must have stamina and the climbing ability of a Matterhorn guide. His is an arduous life fraught with a certain amount of peril—and a large proportion of India's shikaris bear scars made by claws of the tiger.

The Pere David's deer *(Elaphurus davidianus),* rarest of all deer, existed in the Imperial Park in Peking and was discovered by the Abbe David in 1865. The Chinese called it *Mi-lou* or *ssw-pw-hsiang,* which means "four unlike characters." Today they exist only in zoos and private herds.

The giant panda *(Ailuropoda melanoleuca)* is an extremely rare mammal found in the mountains of Szechwan and Kansu in Western China and on the Tibetan Plateau. A cousin of the bear and the coati, his diet consists of fish, small mammals, grasses, roots, plants, bulbs, and bamboo shoots.

The Indian rhinoceros *(Rhinoceros unicornis)*, much larger in body than the common African rhino, is on the road to extinction. At present there are perhaps less than 600 left in all of Nepal, Bengal, and Assam.

The Indian lion *(Panthera leo persica)* was once common but now exists only in the Gir Forest Sanctuary. A census in 1950 indicated that there were 240 lions in the 500-square-mile preserve. Now there are 177.

EUROPE

President Tito of Yugoslavia (opposite) with a magnificent specimen of the huge Carpathian stag shot by him in the pine forests of Belje.

Photograph by Peter Barrett

EUROPE has nothing as exotic as the Bengal tiger of India. It boasts no dangerous game comparable to the mighty African elephant, rhino, Cape buffalo, and tawny lion. It hasn't anywhere near the variety of big game to be found in North America, nor any animal to match the big Kenai moose, the wapiti or the mammoth Kodiak bear.

What it does have—red deer, fallow deer, roebuck, wild boar, ibex, and chamois—it loves with a passion. The serious European big-game hunter pursues his favorite quarry with a fanatical zeal unrivaled in Nimrods of other lands.

It's nothing new. It's been going on for centuries and the pace was set by sundry Princes, Kings, Emperors, and Electors in the Middle Ages. The Electors of Saxony, owing to their ancient and hereditary claim to the title of "Lord High Masters of the Chase for the Holy Roman Empire," enjoyed exceptional opportunities to hunt and apparently dropped everything when the great thick-necked stags began to roar up on the wooded slopes. During the 24-year period of his reign one of these rulers, Elector John George II of Saxony, shot an astounding total of 42,649 red deer. It was done, moreover, with a heavy muzzle-loading gun. A wheel-lock, its spring had to be wound up like a clock and eventually, after the trigger was pulled, the weapon would fire when the serrated edge of the wheel struck enough spark from the piece of pyrites pressing against it. Heaven alone knows what a total John George might have run up if he'd been equipped with a bolt-action Mauser and unlimited cartridges.

It was this same Elector who once turned down the crown of Bohemia, not for political reasons but simply because the Bohemian stags were inferior in size. To make sure that nobody else shot any of *his* stags he built a high and very expensive fence around the entire boundary between Saxony and Bohemia.

There were many other rulers equally eager.

Louis XIII of France was a devotee of the chase as well as a serious gun collector who, by the time he was 14, owned 50 fine arquebuses made by the greatest gunsmiths of Europe. He not only knew how to use them but could take them apart and repair them like a master armorer.

Louis XV was such a rabid hunting maniac that he even stopped on the way home from his coronation to hunt in the Villers-Cotterets Forest in 1722. It just happened to be St. Hubert's Day, and Hubert happens to be patron saint to most venery-minded Europeans. Three years later, in 1725, the King actually managed to spend 276 days out of that year hunting.

His successor, Louis XVI, who later lost his head on the guillotine, was happily hunting on the day the Bastille was stormed. It was a bad day because he had not bagged so much as a rabbit.

An early Landgrave of Hesse had a codicil added to the Lord's Prayer. The additional line went: "Give us this day our daily hart in the pride of grease," the latter bit meaning a stag taken in fat condition during the month preceding the rut.

And it wasn't just the men who were trigger happy.

The ladies, from duchesses to empresses, were also mad for the chase. Princess Frederica of Eisenach was famous for her skill at deer-stalking, while Maria, Governess of the Netherlands, could track her stag, grass it neatly with a crossbow and then, rolling up her sleeves, proceed to gralloch her trophy. France had many queens who enjoyed the hunt and it also had Diane de Poitiers, a charmer of many talents who entered into a hunt with zest. One of the treasures she prized was an ivory hunting horn carved for her by the great Benvenuto Cellini. On it he depicted his luscious Nymph of Fontainebleau, the same he had executed in bronze for François I.

Handsomest shooting-box in France, the Chateau de Chenonceau where Diane de Poitiers loved to hunt with Henri II. She posed as Diana for the ivory hunting horn (below) carved by the great and versatile Benvenuto Cellini, the Florentine.

Most of the rulers who still occupied thrones during the early part of this century were almost as avid about hunting as their counterparts of the Middle Ages. Franz Joseph, Emperor of Austria-Hungary, had a great passion for hunting and was still bagging his stag when a very old man. Crown Prince Rudolph, later to die so tragically at Mayerling, was also an accomplished huntsman and in one brief morning at Keszthely stalked and shot 18 roe deer.

The Hapsburgs were quite a shooting family. In 1899 the Archduke Franz Ferdinand in three days of hunting killed 66 record-class roebuck.

Kaiser Wilhelm of Germany, in days prior to World War I, hunted with great shooting parties in the royal forests of Letzlingen and Schorfheide, enjoyed going after enormous wild boar armed only with a boar spear, and on one red-letter day shot a marvellous 44-point stag. His son, Crown Prince Willy, roamed the world hunting big game in his youth.

Italy's King Humbert, whose favorite weapon was a .450 Holland & Holland Express, killed 50 excellent ibex rams each year inside a fortnight, fine shooting in anybody's game book.

The Spanish monarchs were also adept with the rifle and keen huntsmen, and at one Royal Shoot at Picos de Europa in September of 1912 eleven guns killed 81 chamois, close to an all-time record for the past hundred years. Spain is very proud of its red deer, ibex, and wild boar, and one of the most enthusiastic hunters is General Franco.

As for Russia, the czars had superb big-game hunting and in September 1900, in the Imperial Forest of Bialowieza, a 12-day shoot ended with a remarkable bag: 42 bison, 36 elk, 53 red deer stags, 325 roebucks, and 138 wild boars. One would gather that nobody's gunbarrels became too cold. One particular type of hunting much in favor in Russia was coursing after the gray wolf with a pack of borzois.

Something still remains of those days when royalty made hunting a way of life. It is still seen in the uniforms and badges of the gamekeepers and in the quaint rituals and ceremonies which have survived our entrance into this streamlined jet age. It is these very centuries of tradition which are responsible for making Europe one of the most colorful and interesting continents on which one is privileged to hunt today.

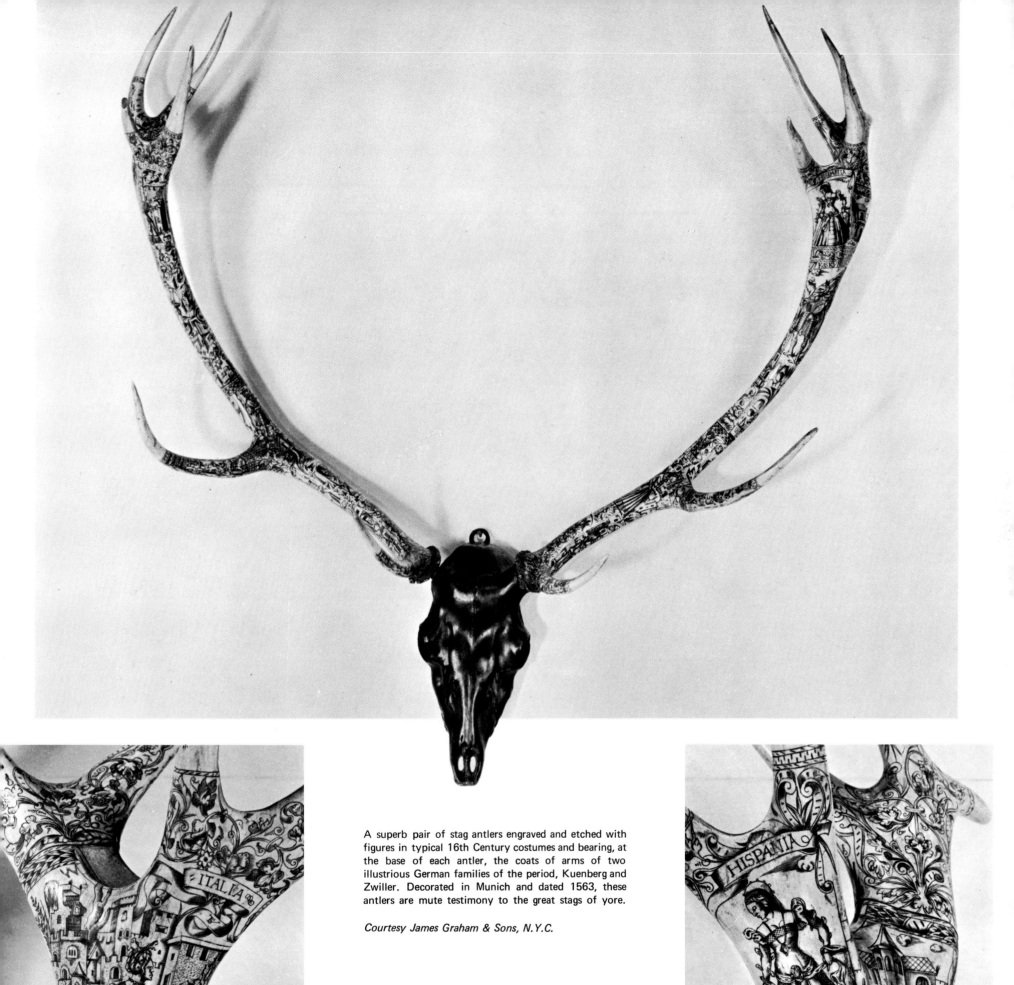

A superb pair of stag antlers engraved and etched with figures in typical 16th Century costumes and bearing, at the base of each antler, the coats of arms of two illustrious German families of the period, Kuenberg and Zwiller. Decorated in Munich and dated 1563, these antlers are mute testimony to the great stags of yore.

Courtesy James Graham & Sons, N.Y.C.

The red deer of Great Britain and Europe *(Cervus elaphus)* is a classic game animal immortalized in song and story. A landowner of vast Scottish moors, the Laird of Invercauld, A.A.C. Farquharson, returns from the heights (opposite) to which he had climbed to glass his great herds of red deer.

THE CHAMOIS

To a European hunter few sporting trophies outrank their own little chamois, a nimble beast of the Alps which averages about seventy pounds and zoologically stands midway between the antelope family and a wild goat. The closest an Austrian can get to heaven and still brag about it is to cleanly kill a trophy chamois buck after a fair and hazardous solo stalk.

To be able to decorate his Tyrolean hat with a *gamsbart*, a cluster of long dark hairs from a crest running from neck to rump, many a Mittel-Europa sportsman has taken his life in his hands to scale near-vertical slopes at dizzying altitudes. Even sixty years ago such a "brush," with hairs eight inches long or better, would bring the equivalent of $50.

The chamois' horns, which are black and cylindrical in cross section, rise straight up from the top of the skull to terminate in distinctive hooks, the record specimen taping in the neighborhood of twelve inches on the front curve.

The chamois has always been the favorite trophy of royalty and one of the most zealous chamois hunters was the old Emperor Franz Joseph, who accounted for 1,991 of them in a 52-year span, using double-barreled rifles made by Springer of Vienna. The world's record for a single chamois drive was made in August of 1892 when Prince Auersperg and his guests killed ninety-four on a private preserve in the Zillerthal.

Many of the wealthier nobles of the Austro-Hungarian Empire prided themselves on their preserves, but since the chamois has always been the prize plum of the poacher, they had a serious problem. One way of solving that problem was reasonably simple and very effective: they merely hired the roughest, toughest poacher in their bailiwick to serve as keeper—and that was that.

The agility and sureness of foot of the chamois are legendary, and they can balance on the tiniest of outcroppings with all the assurance of a ballerina. When climbing they ascend an almost vertical rock face with incredible ease, but when descending they pick their way carefully, unless there is a heavy layer of snow, when they have been known to toboggan down, all four legs forward, like a small boy on a sled.

The range of this interesting and wary mountain denizen ranges from the Pyrenees to the Caucasus, and from the Carpathians to Albania, but Austria has always been the classic place to hunt them, particularly on the Tyrolean peaks.

B. Schocher, Pontresina

THE JAEGER

THE German or Austrian *jaeger*, or hunting guide, is a Man of Distinction in his own community and his diligence to duty is the reason there is still game to be found in the forests and on the alpine heights in Central Europe.

The *jaeger* is usually a man of robust health capable of scaling the perilous rock walls where the chamois and ibex gather. He must be thoroughly familiar with the entire area within his domain and know the habits and haunts of the wildlife in that section— stag, roebuck, chamois, ibex, wild boar. Part of his job is dealing with predators, and he has the power to arrest poachers. It is his responsibility to keep a census of the game within his area and report it to the proper government bureau. In some districts he is required to train and keep a hunting dog, usually a Bavarian Gebirgshund or a Hanoverian Schweiss- hund, to track down any animal hit in the jaw, leg, or other nonfatal place. Among his special talents will be the calling of roebuck in rutting season with a blade of grass or a rubber squeaker, and it is he who will construct a rustic *hochsitz*, a shooting plat- form up in a tree at a height which prevents human scent from being carried to the animal being stalked. Used mostly for roe deer, the platform enables a hunter to assess the size of the antlers before making the shot, and the tree itself yields a steady support for his weapon.

It is the *jaeger* who perpetuates the ancient cus- toms of the hunt such as the *letzter bissen* and the *schützenbruch*.

The *letzter bissen* was probably originally based on the Last Supper, and consists of the *jaeger* put- ting a leafed twig of pine or larch in the mouth of dead cloven-hoofed game such as a red deer stag or European elk. The *schützenbruch* is a branch dipped into the blood of the big-game animal and presented to the hunter on the blade of the forester's knife. In earlier days, when royalty was rampant, the *jae- ger*, on bended knee, presented the *schützenbruch* on top of his battered hunting hat.

Besides his hobnailed boots and keen-edged hunting knife, the *jaeger* always carries an old-fashioned col- lapsible telescope slung over his shoulder in order to estimate the size and antler quality of stags on a distant slope or the age and horn-size of ibex or chamois high in the bergs above. This saves many a fruitless climb.

The fallow deer *(Cervus dama)* is found today in certain sections of Central and Southern Europe, Western Asia as well as in England in private herds. Its range once included Portugal, Spain, Greece, Anatolia, Rhodes, Sardinia, and as far as the Sea of Galilee. The Romans introduced it to Britain.

The author's *jaeger,* in the Austrian Tyrol, slings a chamois trophy like a rucksack to tote him down the mountainslope. In his hat he wears the *gamsbart,* a plume composed of long bristly hairs from the ridge of the spine. Such a "brush" even sixty years ago brought $50 on the market.

In Central Europe the ibex or chamois hunter wears
a Tyrolian jacket and plus-fours of loden, a cloth
virtually rainproof. His mountain boots are cleated
and an alpenstock can be used to steady his aim.

Foto-Flury, Pontresina

The European ibex, or Steinbock (Capra ibex), protected in most of the areas where it still exists, weighs up to 120 pounds. Italy's King Humbert, an excellent shot, once bagged 50 rams in a fortnight.

139

Europe was the cradle of the gun. Kings, emperors, and electors owned weapons more valuable than their crown jewels. The magnificent gun opposite was crafted by a German team, Sadeler and Vischer, for presentation to Henri IV of France. It is a wheel-lock and is ivory inlaid.

Author's Collection

The European bison, or wisent *(Bison bonasus)* seen above once roamed over Central Europe and the Caucasus but today exists only in private preserves such as the Forest of Bialowicsa in Poland, once hunting grounds of Russian czars. It is less shaggy than the buffalo of our plains.

141

The European roebuck is the pixy of the gallery forest, a dainty small deer much prized by all Europeans for its delicious venison. It is hunted by stalking and by waiting in a *hochsitz,* a tree-platform. It can be lured within range by a squeal made blowing through a blade of grass.

The European roebuck (*Capreolus caprea*) is slightly over two feet at the shoulder. A patch of white hairs near the rump will expand when he is alarmed, like the proghorn.

During the 18th and 19th centuries in Central Europe, before taxidermy, chamois, roebuck and stag trophies were inset into skillfully carved wooden heads, sometimes painted. Here is a chamois (left) and a roebuck.

The Sardinian mouflon (*Ovis musimon*), the curly-horned sheep native to the mountains of Corsica and Sardinia, is one of the handsomest of wild sheep of the world, although smaller than most.

The European brown bear (*Ursus arctus*) is famed for his tricks in circuses, particularly riding motor scooters. He once ranged over Switzerland, France, Britain, and parts of Scandinavia. A big one might tape eight feet and weigh 300 pounds, but the Russian variety grows very much bigger.

The wolf is the largest wild member of the dog tribe and exists in Europe, Asia, and America. The last wolf in England was killed in 1743 in Sutherlandshire and a few can still be found in parts of Central Europe and in numbers in Siberia where they band together into enormous packs.

The European wild boar grows to huge size and can be extremely savage if brought to bay, ripping a man repeatedly with razor-sharp tushes well adapted for such mayhem.

NORTH AMERICA

Mel Johnson of Peoria, Illinois, with his world record whitetail deer shot with bow and arrow. Taken in fair chase, it scored 204 4/8 points.

OPPOSITE: Typical Eastern whitetail buck of medium body size with poor but shapely antlers.

INDIA boasts of its tigers and its exotic temples; Africa owns a brace of formidable heavyweights, the rhino and elephant; Europe is bursting with *Gemütlichkeit*, palaces, and traditions—but North America begrudges none of it. It takes pride in having some of the most coveted big-game trophies in the whole world in astounding quantity and variety. There's that earthquake that walks like a bear, the Kodiak; the immense Kenai moose; the wapiti, or American elk, whose mighty antlers would shame the finest Carpathian staghead, and a great quartet of deer numbering in millions. Wild and wary sheep exist in four flavors; there's a big and handsome white mountain goat unlike anything else in the world, and a pronghorn antelope of the arid deserts equally unique on the globe. Arctic denizens there are, also—the walrus, polar bear, musk-ox, and three kinds of caribou. Just for contrast there is a savage tropic terror, the grim jaguar of the Mexican and Yucatan jungles, and a medium-size wild pig, the peccary, or javelina. To this list must be added that most typical of all American game animals, the shaggy bison of the western plains as well as the Canadian northwest. Two or more types of bears occur, too—the mountain grizzly, fully as dangerous as any African lion, and the black bear with his cinnamon and glacier color phases. The puma, or cougar, is found in reasonable quantities from Mexico far up into British Columbia on the western side of the continent.

What makes North America such a dynamic and challenging continent to hunt is the ever-changing backdrop, scenery ranging from bamboo jungles in the south to ice floes and glaciers in the north, while in between lie the sunbaked deserts of Arizona, hotter than the Sahara; the cool timbered mountain slopes of California, Idaho and the West Coast; the rugged terrain of Colorado; the wilds of Idaho; the northwoods of Canada; the forbidding swamps of the Southeast, and bucolic farming country which has managed to produce some recent deerheads that have knocked the record books silly. Few visitors have failed to be awed by the majestic grandeur of British Columbia, the Yukon and Alaska where the great mountain ranges and limitless horizons make a six-footer feel a pygmy.

Yes, there are not only some superb and crafty trophy animals but also a rugged, wonderful wilderness immortalized by James Oliver Curwood, Rex Beach, Jack London, and a poet, Robert W. Service.

Year in and year out, the most popular animal of North America, the one which the greatest number of hunters seek, is the whitetail deer. In the U.S.A. alone over a million are taken each year, and it is a tribute to conservation departments and their allies that there are today more deer in this country than existed at the time of Daniel Boone. The state of Texas alone has a deer population of over two million and Pennsylvania has over 600,000 whitetails.

What is also remarkable is that bigger deer and better heads are found now than at the turn of the century. What's more, the best trophies are coming not from the wild, wild northwoods but from farming districts fairly well populated. The current world record whitetail, for instance, was taken with a bow and arrow in a soybean field just outside the city limits of Peoria, Illinois. A 12-pointer, it dressed out at 270 pounds, scored 204 4/8 points by Boone and Crockett standards, and was bagged by Mel Johnson, a young hunter who had gone far afield in Wisconsin, Pennsylvania, Colorado, and Missouri in his attempts to find a decent rack during previous seasons.

The first man to successfully bag a trophy head of every major species of North American big game was my old friend, the late Grancel Fitz, who worked at that goal with the zest of Galahad seeking the Holy Grail. Today, with jet planes shrinking the map, a few others have accomplished the same, but Grancel was Number One.

The two houseboats and gasboat caught like grebes in the ice in the sudden freeze-up on the Wolf River in Northern Ontario.

GENESIS

FOR me it all began forty years ago in rugged bush on the Wolf River in northern Ontario wilderness, in a white world of swirling snow and freezing sleet. It began with the bagging of the Wolf River buck, a big whitetail patriarch whose craftiness had made him a local legend, a beast almost as elusive as the fabled *loup-garou* of the French Canadians.

He was hardly what you'd call a record-class trophy by modern standards but to me he looked big as a bull moose and when he dropped flat at the crack of my little iron-sighted .303 I wasn't just a deerhunter any longer.

No sir-ree. I was a big-game hunter.

Then and there it became my intention to spend as much of the rest of my life as possible looking for bigger and better trophies, and what that enthusiasm has cost me since would buy a gross of Rolls-Royces, a ton of beluga caviar, and forty cases of Dom Pérignon champagne.

What it brought me in the way of pleasure, excitement, challenge, and adventure over those decades can never be estimated in the prosaic terms of cold cash.

There's another reason I remember the Wolf River buck.

Pound for pound, he was the most expensive chunk of venison I've *ever* toted home.

Ours was the first group to try Archie Rogerson's new homemade houseboat as a mobile base camp for a deer hunt. Slapped together, with a cabin of unpainted boards, it wasn't exactly a luxury yacht and yet it was comfortable. The cars in which we had come were left behind at the old dock at Port Loring, their radiators drained although the weather was unseasonably warm. There was no tang to the air, no hint of frost, and it seemed like anything but the kind of weather in which to hunt antlered bucks on the long brown ridges.

We made slow progress chugging up the Pickerel River and on into the Wolf, eventually anchoring alongside Archie's personal houseboat which he'd towed up a week before in order to stake a claim on that particular section of deer country, a prize area.

Next morning we were out at dawn, combing the surrounding territory. We hiked all day, had a couple

of desultory drives, and the only deer we saw were some does hightailing into a cedar swamp far to the north. It might as well have been Indian Summer, and we were perspiration-soaked at the end of a grueling day.

Overnight the temperature dropped fifty degrees. I was awakened by the chattering of teeth all around me and finally we drew straws to see who'd erupt from his blankets to start a fire in the potbelly stove. A pitcher of water on a pine table had a half-inch of ice on top and through the window we could see snowflakes big as mothballs.

Both boats were frozen solid and we attacked the ice with axes and peevie poles in an attempt to free them.

It was useless.

"Leave 'em be," said Archie. "We haven't the equipment necessary, so when it comes time to depart I'll send a runner out for a tug to break the ice."

In the week that we hunted, with more snow falling every day, we managed to bag our legal allotment, my share of which was the Wolf River buck.

Henry Rogerson set off on foot to a fire tower to put in a call for a tug, which got stuck in the ice. A second tug got lost in a blizzard. A phone call to Pakesley finally got us the promise of a gasboat to pick us up at an open stretch on the swifter-flowing Pickerel, ten or twelve miles to the north. A lumber teamster, a dour Scot, hauled our deer out for us as we slogged through the deep snow on foot.

The point was bleak and windswept, with the temperature hovering near zero, and it was seven that night before we made out the vague shape of a gasboat offshore in a driving blizzard. It didn't see us, and being upwind in the teeth of an Arctic gale, was unable to hear our frantic shots.

A passing lumber barge finally saw our flares and picked us up. He was going the wrong way but he got no argument from us and, frozen from exposure in the open boat, we disembarked at Lost Channel. Finally, two days later, we decided to hire a sort of Rube Goldberg lumber locomotive to haul us and our stack of deer carcasses to Pakesley, a dot on the map many miles still farther north from our destination. From that place we boarded a train to Sudbury on the Soo Line, still farther afield, and two more trains to North Bay and Trout Creek, where we hired a sleigh.

By that time we had hauled our venison over 400 miles to get back to our cars which, as the crow flies, were less than 25 miles from the houseboats.

The meat from the Wolf River buck cost me roughly $20 per pound, and being of Scottish descent I almost choked on every morsel.

Alaska's Kenai moose *(Alces gigas)* is one of the finest big-game animals in the world. Found mainly on Kenai Peninsula, a full-grown bull might weigh 1,400 pounds. The record-book trophy, opposite, was bagged by Warren Page, Shooting Editor of *Field & Stream*, while hunting in the Moose Creek section of Ptarmigan Valley, east of Rainy Pass. The spread was 72 inches — and the score 215 7/8.

The World's Record Moose (above) was bagged by Bert Klineburger on Mt. Susitna, Alaska, after four seasons without success. This superb head, of 77 4/8 inch spread, scored 251.

The remarkably massive moose antlers at left were acquired by the Field Museum of Natural History of Chicago in the last quarter of the 19th Century. A sensation at the time, these horns have been bettered by modern sportsmen.

THE MILLAIS ANTLERS

THIS famous pair of Alaskan moose antlers, of record-book size, involved two noted sportsmen. The trophy was bagged by St. George Littledale, a fabulous marksman who was England's No. 1 big-game hunter. He presented them to his good friend, J. G. Millais, a noted hunter himself and one of the finest painters of animals and birds in the world, author of the African classic *A Breath from the Veldt*. Millais carefully scraped the antlers down to the white and proceeded to embellish them, in semi-scrimshaw technique, with magnificent drawings of the big game of Northern America—the moose, bison, wapiti, grizzly, bighorn sheep, black bear, mountain goat, a Dall ram, as well as Indians, totems, and foxes. Fired up by his enthusiasm, he then covered the *backs* of the palms with caribou, pronghorn antelopes, charging grizzly, a herd of buffalo, mule deer bucks, and cowboys roping. As a final touch he covered the tines, fore and aft, with over a hundred ducks and geese including all species native to North America. The extreme spread of these antlers is 65¼ inches and they constitute a unique tribute to the big game of our continent.

A straw-colored mountain grizzly sow from the high slopes of the Alaska Range tugs at a succulent vine in her quest for food. This platinum-blonde variety is known to guides as a "Jean Harlow," digs up ground squirrels for a snack.

Just such a big and savage grizzly as the one on the opposite page killed two girl campers in Glacier Park in 1967 without provocation of any kind. Just prior to hibernation such an animal might weigh 1,000 pounds, and in attacking might claw a man, gnaw on him, and drag him off to his den.

ABOVE: A big Alaskan brown bear in heavy spring pellage, unrubbed, bagged by the author on Chichagof Island, 1940.

LEFT: A very big Alaskan brown bear in April with coat badly rubbed from much scraping against trees and rocks after emerging from long hibernation with an itchy skin.

Above, two hungry Kodiaks argue possession of a salmon in midstream. In July when these fish migrate into the streams to spawn, the giant bears gather at the riffles like housewives at a supermarket. On the opposite page is a three-quarters-of-a-ton bear — a monster meat-eater.

160

A happy-go-lucky blonde grizzly comes out to feed (above) then hears the click of the camera (opposite) and becomes less amiable. If pressed too close, such a bear may charge.

LEND-LEASE ANIMALS

THE woods bison (above) and the musk-ox (opposite) exist today in Alaska and parts of Canada because of intelligent transplanting and strict protection for an extended period of time. The woods bison now has made a fine comeback in Woods Bison National Park in Canada's Northwest Territory where it roams an area almost as large as Nova Scotia. In 1928 twenty-three bison were transplanted from Montana to Big Delta, a spot 90 miles southeast of Fairbanks, where they have thrived in similar fashion.

The last native North American musk-ox (*Ovibos moschatus niphoecus*) was killed in Alaska in 1865. The Eskimos hunted "Oomingmuk" for winter meat as well as for the deep-pile wool, called *qiviut*, from which they wove superlative blankets. In 1930 a herd of 34 musk-oxen was transplanted from Greenland to Nunivak Island in the Bering Sea, where they have multiplied. Although they have no natural enemies on this island, their survival is now threatened by depletion of natural forage.

A distant cousin of the Asiatic serow and takin, a musk-ox bull will tape three-and-a-half feet at the shoulder and weigh up to 900 pounds. When attacked by wolves, musk-oxen form a tight circle with bulls and old cows shoulder to shoulder in a phalanx bristling with horns to protect the calves and yearlings.

OPPOSITE: The giant Alaskan brown bear (*Ursus arctos middendorffi*) is three times the weight of an African lion and can be fully as savage.

LEFT: Lee Considine, veteran Alaskan guide, was one of the early specialists on Brownies.

THE ALASKAN GUIDE

LIKE the white hunter of Africa, the Alaskan guide is a highly paid, able and gutty character. Only the cream of the crop get their names on the Alaskan Registered Guide list and of these perhaps a dozen veterans have achieved world-wide fame through guiding kings, emperors, millionaires, and noted international sportsmen.

To qualify for the Registered Guide list a man must have a minimum of five years' experience in trapping and hunting in the Alaskan wilderness. He must pass a written test based on his knowledge of wildlife, firearms, and game laws. He must be in tiptop shape physically to withstand the rigors of tramping muskeg and climbing to the rugged peaks where mountain goat and wild sheep range. His aim must be deadly with a rifle to save a tenderfoot client from the attack of a grizzly, brown bear, or even an angry cow moose with calf. He must know how to live off the land in case a marauding bear or wolverine has found and robbed his cache of food, and he is expected to know much about first aid in the event of accident. Many registered Alaskan guides today are expert bush pilots and as a result are able to take their paying customers back into country rarely if ever hunted. Due mainly to this feature of modern hunting technique, record heads and skulls are coming out of the back country to beat the best that Alaska produced even in its infancy when it was truly America's last frontier.

The Alaska Registered Guide is usually as handy with a camera as with a gun, since today the camera-hunters are as numerous as the riflemen. Some guides specialize on two of the extraordinary beasts of which Alaska is so proud—the giant Kenai moose and the equally big brown bear, an incredible brute three times as heavy as the African lion and fully as savage. An all-Alaska guide is rare, for he must know his way in treacherous muskeg and on mountain peak; he must know tides like a master mariner, and the ice floes, while after polar bear and walrus, like an Eskimo. He works hard for his wages and wouldn't change places with a king.

THE WAPITI

ALTHOUGH the Indian name, wapiti, is correct, this enormous member of the deer family is usually called elk—although technically that term belongs to the skimpy-antlered "moose" of Europe. When early white travelers penetrated the eastern part of North America they found the elk where Pennsylvania, Ohio, and New York now lie. Today the best hunting areas would include the Selway and Salmon River sections of Idaho, Montana's Bitterroots, Alberta's Brazeau River, Wyoming's famed Jackson Hole, and Arizona's Apache Indian Reservation near White River.

The elk is a huge and majestic beast weighing well over 1,000 pounds in many instances, with massive antlers which have caused sportsmen all over the globe to rate him a superb trophy. A record-book elk head will dwarf the finest Carpathian stag.

The elk is migratory, can swim well and can jump a 7½-foot fence when in the mood. A bull will service as many as fifteen cows in his herd and even romance a domestic cow for variety. In the fall elk herd up and it is then that the rutting bull bugles his challenge to his rivals, and sportsmen who have witnessed a battle never forget it. An able guide can whistle a shrill tremolo call which brings a bull on the run.

Photograph by Alaska Film

The Pacific walrus *(Odobenus divergens)* grows to a length of 13 feet and might weigh up to a ton-and-a-half. He uses his tusks to dig mussels out of the muck and his only enemy other than man is the orca, the killer whale. Eskimos prize his dark flesh, make raincoats from his intestines.

AT LEFT: Bert Klineburger with a very large bull walrus.

The polar bear *(Thalarctos maritimus)* is the largest of all bears, weighs up to 1600 pounds and will attack men.

The male polar bear is a loner, a restless nomad that prowls the ice fields in quest of a seal dinner and never hibernates. His big feet are broad and hairy with nonslip pads, and he is a strong and tireless swimmer. He roams the Arctic areas of Alaska, Europe, Canada, Russia, and Greenland.

RIGHT: Charles H. Stoll, veteran big-game hunter, with a monster polar bear estimated at 1800 pounds bagged fifty miles west of Point Hope in the Arctic ice pack when Stoll was 70 years old.

THE WAPITI

The Roosevelt elk (Cervus c. roosevelti) above is the largest of the elk and roams the rain-forests of the northwest Pacific coastal area.

ALTHOUGH the Indian name, wapiti, is correct, this enormous member of the deer family is usually called elk—although technically that term belongs to the skimpy-antlered "moose" of Europe. When early white travelers penetrated the eastern part of North America they found the elk where Pennsylvania, Ohio, and New York now lie. Today the best hunting areas would include the Selway and Salmon River sections of Idaho, Montana's Bitterroots, Alberta's Brazeau River, Wyoming's famed Jackson Hole, and Arizona's Apache Indian Reservation near White River.

The elk is a huge and majestic beast weighing well over 1,000 pounds in many instances, with massive antlers which have caused sportsmen all over the globe to rate him a superb trophy. A record-book elk head will dwarf the finest Carpathian stag.

The elk is migratory, can swim well and can jump a 7½-foot fence when in the mood. A bull will service as many as fifteen cows in his herd and even romance a domestic cow for variety. In the fall elk herd up and it is then that the rutting bull bugles his challenge to his rivals, and sportsmen who have witnessed a battle never forget it. An able guide can whistle a shrill tremolo call which brings a bull on the run.

The late Grancel Fitz bagged the fine bison bull (above) on a special permit and became the first man to ever shoot all major species of North American big-game. My photograph of Grancel (right) was taken at the Camp Fire Club of America.

America's most typical game animal, the buffalo of the Old West, *(Bison bison)* once existed in numbers estimated at sixty million, yet by the end of the century they were almost extinct due to the depradations of the hide hunters. Under intelligent protection they have made a comeback. A bull might weigh 2200 pounds.

The mountain goat *(Oreamnos kennedyi* weighing up to 300 pounds, has a temper like a tarantula and will take on a timber wolf. The Chilkat Indians made robes from his wool.

Only wild white sheep in the world, the Dall sheep *(Ovis dalli)* might weigh 225 pounds and has eyes like an eagles, sharp ears, and poor sense of smell. Alaska is his habitat.

Photos above by Cecil Rhode

One of the greatest American big game rifles was the Winchester Model 1873, having a magazine holding twelve husky .44/40 cartridges. This handsome one, from the author's collection, is the Special Sporting Rifle engraved at the factory by Ulrich for a presentation.

Pound for pound, the North American jaguar *(Felis onca hernadesii)* is the most dangerous beast on our continent, as fierce as the African leopard and much heavier. His nemesis for years was Frank Colcord (above), famed hunter who guided me into Sonora's *cajons* after jaguar.

Second largest mountain lion ever to be bagged is this whopper I took in Sonora while hunting with Colcord's Tonto Rim pack of lion and bear dogs to which any puma or jaguar was a pussycat.

The timber wolf is one of the most cunning of all predators and his exceptional vision, hearing and high-powered nose allow him to elude man with ease. Top weight would be 120 pounds.

The western mule deer is one of the handsomest North American trophies, being big in body and bearing superb antlers, wide spread and massive. This beauty was bagged by writer Peter Barrett.

Photo by Peter Barrett

ABOVE: He who hunts bear in Alaska in the spring should be prepared to dress like a halibut fisherman, since it rains buckets. The tide flat you walk across in the morning may have twelve feet of water over it in the afternoon.

LEFT: A big record-book Alaskan black bear, taken in the spring of 1940. Itinerant base camp was the yacht *Caroline*.

CARL RUNGIUS

THE finest painter of North America's big game was the late great Carl Rungius, a German who arrived in New York at the turn of the century to do animal drypoints and etchings, then began to do oil paintings. By 1908 he was already famous for his "Rainbow Rams on Lava Peak," which was reproduced in color as the frontispiece to William T. Hornaday's *Camp Fires on Desert and Lava*.

A year or two later he made a trip into the wilderness of the Upper Yukon with a noted big-game hunter, Charles Sheldon, and at one time their campfire was shared by Frederick Courtenay Selous, then the most famous of the African professional hunters.

Rungius hunted every species of moose in North America and bagged some notable heads high in the record class. He had no time for such newfangled gadgets as telescopic sights, and his best shot with iron sights, he once confided to me, was not at big game at all but one which killed a wolverine on the carcass of a caribou bull at 250 yards.

Rungius was a tireless worker, and on a hunt would make hundreds of sketches of game in action as well as details of the terrain, and no other artist has ever packed so much knowledge and accuracy into the representation of a moose, grizzly, sheep, pronghorn antelope, or mountain goat.

When I last talked to Carl, then eighty-five years of age, he was preparing to return to Canada to hunt moose and grizzly in his favorite country, the wild area north of Banff, where his main studio had been.

SOUTH AMERICA

The late Grancel Fitz, veteran big-game hunter, with an Indian blackbuck bagged in Argentina, a better head than he found during a hunt in India.

ONCE upon a time, light years ago in the dim, dark past, South America possessed a plethora of enormous beasts—the saber-toothed tiger, huge lions, mastodons, mylodons big as a white rhinoceros, and a giant ground sloth with claws like sickles. As the result of some subterranean upheaval or similar catastrophe, all of these creatures vanished in mysterious fashion, and today South America can claim only three truly indigenous animals which qualify as big game: the great jaguar of Brazil and Paraguay, the spectacled bear of the high Andes, and a puma identical with our North American species. Neither the guanaco nor the tapir are regarded seriously as big-game trophies.

This does not mean that South America is suffering from a shortage of big game. As a matter of fact, it has a great abundance in a dozen flavors and a wide variety of antler and horn styles—but they are not natives. These are all exotics, beasts from other continents transplanted to South America with great success. Not only have these immigrants thrived in Argentina and elsewhere, but in many cases they have produced better heads than in their homeland.

It was back in 1906 that a shipment of red deer and wild boar of the Carpathians was imported by Pedro Luro, followed by fallow deer from England and axis deer and blackbuck from India. The idea caught on in much the same manner as has the importation of Barbary sheep into Texas in recent years. Much of the best hunting is on privately owned land, naturally, but there are outfitters in Buenos Aires who can make arrangements for the visiting sportsman. Husky European boars, great trophies and exciting to hunt, can in some sections be shot without license or limit.

The scarcity of indigenous big game in South America didn't bother old Teddy Roosevelt when he joined Colonel Rondon there, in 1915, in an attempt to solve the mystery of the River of Doubt.

Traversing 900 miles of grim jungle and swamp, the ex-President of the United States faced manifold dangers from deadly snakes, piranhas, treacherous rapids, fever, fatigue, and malnutrition. He and Kermit took in their stride the attacks of ticks, fire-ants, leeches, mosquitoes, gnats, *maribundi* wasps, vicious bloodsucking *boroshuda* flies, and the awful *berni* fly

which deposits eggs in living creatures. Somehow, between fighting off these myriad pests, Teddy and his son found time to kill jaguar, marsh deer, tapir, a giant anteater called *tamandua bandeira*, as big as a black bear and prone to attack if cornered, monkeys, and the *capybara*, a semi-aquatic guinea pig the size of a beaver. To Teddy it was bully—simply bully.

Some truly extraordinary trophies have been taken in South America in recent years. On one of his last hunts the late Grancel Fitz took record-class blackbuck and stag there, and the Seattle taxidermist-hunter Bert Klineberger bagged an Indian buffalo (*Bos bubalus*) in Brazil, on Marajó Island at the mouth of the Amazon, far better than you could expect to come upon in India. Outdoor-writer Peter Barrett, within the past year, shot a much better axis deer (*Cervus axis*) there than I was able to find in all of Madhya Pradesh at approximately the same time.

Of the imports, the most dangerous would be the Indian buffalo and the European boar. The great jaguar of Paraguay and Brazil can be dangerous indeed when given provocation, for he has both the weight and the weapons to kill a cow or a man. The puma, a relatively harmless predator in North America, has been known to attack man in Southern Patagonia.

It was in Patagonia, fifty or sixty years ago, that an unusual form of hunting was traditional. The hunters were the Tehuelche Indians, tall picturesque men who rode unshod ponies with the zeal of Cossacks and thrust boots of guanaco leather into silver stirrups. Each hunter was mounted on his best horse and kept a spare mount following at the end of a rawhide rope. Hunting in pairs, the riders spread in all directions to form an immense circle into the center of which they methodically drove all game and eventually, in the eye of this hurricane of activity, there would be huddled together hundreds of guanacos, ostriches, and possibly even a puma or two, all of which the Indians would attack with bolas and with clubs, dismounting to leap onto the victims with frenzied ferocity. For sheer mass carnage it was exceeded only by the rabbit drives of Australia.

OPPOSITE: South America's finest big game—the jaguar of the Matto Grosso, bigger than a leopard.

TIGER MAN

Through the steaming jungles and stinking swamps of the Mato Grosso, in Brazil, roams the mightiest cat of the Americas, a magnificent carnivore with hide of burnished gold speckled with blue-black rosettes. He might outweigh the biggest African leopard by a hundred pounds, has massively muscled shoulders, and one swat from his lethal paw can kill a full-grown steer. Ranchers curse him for his forays into their cattle, and natives dread the man-killers spawned by his clan. He is the South American jaguar, called *el tigre*, a cat so large that a pelt from a big male will sometimes cover the hide of an African maned lion. His earth-shaking roar is so frightening in volume that some lone hunters, hearing it at close range, have called off their dogs and returned home.

For decades the nemesis of this bold predator was a bearded white man who lived on the banks of the Miranda River and his accomplishments constitute South America's greatest hunting story.

Sasha Siemel's deeds are so legendary that he has become as famed in his own life span as did Buffalo Bill Cody in the days of our wild, wild West.

When I first met him, twenty years ago, Sasha had been in at the kill of 281 of these big cats. He captured 22 alive and killed 111 with bow and arrow, but his nickname of *Tiger Man* came from his favorite method of killing a jaguar, meeting the charge of the catapulting terror with only a spear for defense. At that time he had slain 30 with his flashing blade—and he went on to kill others.

A Latvian, Siemel wandered into the Mato Grosso in 1918 and spent almost 50 years hunting there. Using a *zagaya*, a husky spear made of *louro* wood with a hand-forged blade a foot long, he learned the technique of this perilous form of sport from a Guato Indian named Joachim.

Based on Sasha's records, three out of ten "tigers" will charge when brought to bay by a pack of hounds. In the case of a female with cubs the ratio jumps to 100 percent. Once he had tried this suicidal method of hunting, he was hooked. There is nothing in the world, he told me, to match the thrill that hits you when that orange mass of muscle and mayhem explodes through the green curtain of foliage straight at you. A one-time Greco-Roman-style wrestler, Sasha Siemel had the perfect physique for handling an oncoming jaguar. The idea is to stand firm-footed but loose-kneed, so that you can aim accurately and yet sidestep fast if necessary. Usually the weight and momentum of the big cat is sufficient to impale itself on the blade, and then with a combined thrust, heave, and a grunt you pitch him over your head like a load of hay. There's a lot of primordial man in Sasha Siemel, a most remarkable and fearless fellow now, regrettably, retired.

Sasha Siemel, above, with a huge 300-pound jaguar, one of thirty such predators he has killed with a spear in his long years in the Matto Grosso jungles. At right is Sasha and Russ Aitken, 20 years ago, in front of a jaguar pelt so big it covered that of an African lion.

One of the most successful of big-game transplants to South America was the red deer of Europe *(Cervus elaphus)* (above) which has thrived and developed some extraordinary antlers.

Veteran big-game hunter and taxidermist, Bert Klineburger, with an enormous record-class Indian buffalo taken in Brazil on Marajo Island at the very mouth of the Amazon River.

Writer-hunter Peter Barrett (at right) with a record-class axis deer *(Cervus axis)* dropped with a long shot near Mar del Plata in the Argentine, better than most shot in India.

The spectacled bear of the Andes (*Ursus ornatus*) is smaller than the North American black bear, and at the turn of the century its range extended down the chain of the Andes from Colombia to Chili and Bolivia. Today the beast is very rare.

The South American peccary has a reputation for ferocity. He gives off a peculiar skunk-like odor, kills good-sized venomous snakes with very little trouble, and hunts in large packs. A big boar might weigh 90 pounds and has savage tusks.

The odd tapir of Brazil and Paraguay *(Tapirus terrestris)* is a sizeable animal whose nose and upper lip form a peculiar flexible trunk. It eats leaves, shoots, and buds, is basically nocturnal, and when pursued takes to the rivers where it swims surprisingly well. A member of the Perissodactyl ungulates, it has undergone little change since the Miocene. A cousin, the pinchaque, lives in the Andes.

Index to illustrations

ABDOREZZA, PRINCE 103
ADDAX (*Addax nasomaculatus*) 88
ALASKAN BROWN BEAR (*Ursus arctos middendorffi*) 167
ALASKAN GUIDE 166
ALASKAN TIDE FLAT 182
ALPINE HUNTING CLOTHES 133
ARGALI (*Ovis ammon*) 109
ARIEL GAZELLE (*Gazella dama*) 88
AUSTRIAN JAEGER 135
AXIS DEER (*Cervus axis*) 95, 100, 120, 189

BARBARY SHEEP (*Ammotragus lervia*) 72, 73
BEARS
    American Black (*Eurarctos americanus*) 182
    Alaskan Brown (*Ursus arctos middendorffi*) 158, 159, 167
    European Brown (*Ursus arctos*) 145
    Grizzly (*Ursus arctos horribilis*) 156, 157, 162, 163
    Himalayan or Indian (*Selenarctos thibetanus*) 94
    Kodiak (*Ursus arctos middendorffi*) 160, 161
    Polar Bear (*Thalarctos maritimus*) 169, 170, 171
    Spectacled (*Ursus ornatus*) 190
BEISA ORYX (*Oryx gazella beisa*) 70
BISON, AMERICAN (*Bison bison*) 174, 175
BISON, WOODS (*Bison bison athabascae*) 164
BISON, INDIAN (*Bibos gaurus*) 116, 117, 119
BLACKBUCK (*Antilope cervicapra*) 184
BLACK RHINOCEROS (*Diceros bicornis*) 30, 31, 32, 33, 34, 35, 38, 40, 41
BLUE BULL (*Boselaphus tragocamelus*) 122
BOAR, WILD (*Sus scrofa*) 147
BONGO (*Boöcerus eurycerus eurycerus*) 86, 87
BOWMAN, FRANK 14
BUFFALO, CAPE (*Syncerus caffer*) 19, 42, 43, 44, 45, 46, 47, 91
BUFFALO, INDIAN (*Bubalus bubalus*) 188

CAMEL, RACING 85
CAMERAS, SAFARI 90
CAMP IN MASAI 11
CARPATHIAN STAG (*Cervus elephus var.*) 128
CARPATHIAN STAG ANTLERS, Decorated 131
CHAMOIS (*Rupicapra tragus*) 134, 137, 143
CHEETAH (*Acinonyx jubatus jubatus*) 25, 92
CHENONCEAU, CHATEAU 130
CLARK, JAMES L. 110
COLCORD, FRANK 178
CONSIDINE, LEE 166
COOCH-BEHAR, Maharajah of 101

DALL SHEEP (*Ovis dalli*) 176
DAMA GAZELLE (*Gazella dama*) 88
DEER
    Axis (*Cervus axis*) 95, 100, 120, 189
    Fallow (*Cervus dama*) 136
    Hog (*Axis porcinus*) 95
    Mule (*Odocoileus hemionus*) 181
    Père David (*Elaphurus davidianus*) 124
    Red (*Cervus elaphus*) 128, 132, 188
    Roebuck (*Capreolus caprea*) 142, 143
    White Tail (*Odocoileus virginianus*) 143, 149, 151
DELANO, FRANK 88

EDINBURGH, DUKE OF 114
ELAND, COMMON (*Taurotragus oryx*) 22
ELAND, GIANT (*Taurotragus derbianus*) 76, 77, 78
ELEPHANT, AFRICAN (*Loxodonta africana*) 48, 49, 50, 51, 52, 53, 54, 55
ELEPHANT, INDIAN (*Elephas maximus*) 101, 115, 118
ELIZABETH II, H.M. QUEEN 114
ELK, AMERICAN (*Cervus c. roosevelti*) 172

EXPLORERS CLUB FLAG 80
FARQUHARSON, A.A.C. 133
FALLOW DEER (*Cervus dama*) 136
FITZ, GRANCEL 174, 184
FOOT SAFARI 82
FRINGE-EARED ORYX (*Oryx gazella callotis*) 71
GAMSBART 127, 137
GATES, ELGIN 109, 111
GAUR (*Bibos gaurus*) 116, 117, 119
GEMSBUCK (*Oryx gazella gazella*) 81
GERENUK (*Litocranius walleri*) 79
GEORGE V, H.M. KING 115
GIANT ELAND (*Taurotragus derbianus*) 76, 77, 78
GIANT SABLE ANTELOPE (*Hippotragus niger variani*) 74, 75
GIANT PANDA (*Ailuropoda melanoleuca*) 125
GIRAFFE (*Giraffa camelopardalis*) 9, 12, 13
GREATER KUDU (*Tragelaphus strepsiceros*) 61, 62, 63
GNU (*Connochaetes taurinus*) 16, 17
GRIZZLY BEAR (*Ursus arctos horribilis*) 156, 157, 162, 163

HASINGER, DAVID 98
HIPPOPOTAMUS (*Hippopotamus amphibius*) 56
HOG DEER (*Axis porcinus*) 95
HOUSEBOAT HUNT CAMP 150
HUNTER'S HARTEBEESTE (*Damaliscus hunteri*) 80

IBEX, ASIATIC (*Capra ibex sibirica*) 102, 105, 106, 107, 113
IBEX, EUROPEAN (*Capra ibex*) 139
IMPALA (*Aepyceros melampus*) 10, 24
INYALA (*Tragelaphus angasii*) 64, 65
IVORY HUNTING HORN 130

JAEGER, AUSTRIAN 135
JAGUAR, North American (*Felix onca hernandesii*) 178
JAGUAR, South American (*Felix onca hernandesii*) 185, 187
JAIPUR, MAHARAJAH OF 114
JOHNSON, MEL 148

KILIMANJARO 9
KLINEBURGER, BERT 168, 177, 188
KODIAK BEAR (*Ursus arctos middendorffi*) 158, 159, 160, 161
KUDU, GREATER (*Tragelaphus strepsiceros*) 61, 62, 63

LAGARDE, JOHN 102
LAIRD OF INVERCAULD 133
LEOPARD, AFRICAN (*Felis pardus*) 57
LEOPARD, SNOW (*Felis uncia*) 112
LION, AFRICAN (*Panthera leo*) 8, 28, 36, 37, 40, 41
LION, INDIAN (*Panthera leo persica*) 127
LION, MOUNTAIN (*Felis concolor hippolestes*) 179
LORD DERBY'S ELAND (*Taurotragus derbianus*) 76, 77, 78
LUNAN, DAVID 16

MAHARAJAH OF COOCH-BEHAR 101
MAHARAJAH OF JAIPUR 114
MANCHURIAN TIGER (*Panthera felis longipilis*) 93
MARCO POLO SHEEP (*Ovis ammon poli*) 110, 111
MARKHOR (*Capra falconeri*) 102
MILLAIS MOOSE ANTLERS 155
MOHAMMEDAN GUNBEARER 94
MOOSE, ALASKAN (*Alces gigas*) 152, 153, 154, 155
MOUFLON, AFRICAN (*Ammotragus lervia*) 72, 73
MOUFLON, SARDINIAN (*Ovis musimon*) 144

MOUNTAIN GOAT (*Oreamnos americanus kennedyi*) 176
MOUNTAIN LION (*Felis concolor hippolestes*) 179
MULE DEER (*Odocoileus hemionus*) 181
MUNTJAC (*Muntiacus muntjac*) 120
MUSKOX (*Ovibos moschatus wardi*) 165

NILGAI (*Boselaphus tragocamelus*) 122
NYALA (*Tragelaphus angasii*) 64, 65

ORYX, BEISA (*Oryx gazella beisa*) 70
ORYX, FRINGE-EARED (*Oryx gazella callotis*) 71
ORYX, SCIMITAR (*Oryx dammah*) 68, 69
OUM CHALOUBA 84
OVIS POLI SHEEP (*Ovis ammon poli*) 110, 111

PANDA, GIANT (*Ailuropoda melanoleuca*) 125
PASANG (*Capra hircus aegagrus*) 103
PECCARY (*Dicotyles tajacu*) 190
PERCIVAL, PHILIP 15
PÈRE DAVID'S DEER (*Elaphurus davidianus*) 124
POLAR BEAR (*Thalarctos maritimus*) 169, 170, 171
PUMA (*Felis concolor hippolestes*) 179

RED DEER (*Cervus elaphus*) 128, 132, 188
RHINOCEROS, BLACK (*Diceros bicornis*) 30, 31, 32, 33, 34, 35, 38, 40, 41
RHINOCEROS, INDIAN (*Rhinoceros unicornis*) 126
RHINOCEROS, WHITE (*Ceratotherium simum*) 29, 34
ROAN ANTELOPE (*Hippotragus equina koba*) 89
ROEBUCK (*Capreolus caprea*) 142, 143
RUNGIUS, CARL 183

SABLE ANTELOPE (*Hippotragus niger*) 58, 59, 60, 63
SABLE ANTELOPE, GIANT (*Hippotragus niger variani*) 74, 75
SAFARI CARS 83
SAKIN (*Capra ibex sibirica*) 102, 104, 105, 106, 107, 113
SARDINIAN MOUFLON (*Ovis musimon*) 114
SCIMITAR ORYX (*Oryx dammah*) 68, 69
SIEMEL, SASHA 186, 187
SHIKARI 123
SNOW LEOPARD (*Felis uncia*) 112
SPECTACLE BEAR (*Tremarctos ornatus*) 190
STEINBOK (*Raphicerus campestris*) 23
STOLL, CHARLES 171

TAHR (*Hemitragus jehamicus*) 113
TAKIN (*Budorcas taxicolor bedfordi*) 108
TAPIR (*Tapirus terrestris*) 191
TIGER, INDIAN (*Felis tigris*) 96, 97, 98, 99, 101, 114, 115
TIGER, MANCHURIAN (*Panthera felis longipilis*) 93
TITO, PRESIDENT 128

WALRUS (*Odobenus divergens*) 168
WAPITI (*Cervus canadensis nelsoni*) 173
WART-HOG (*Phacochoerus aethiopicus*) 26, 27
WATERBUCK (*Kobus ellipsiprymous*) 66, 67
WESTERN ROAN ANTELOPE (*Hippotragus equinus koba*) 89
WHEEL-LOCK RIFLE, ROYAL 140
WHITE-TAIL DEER (*Odocoileus virginianus*) 148, 149, 151
WILD BOAR (*Sus scrofa*) 147
WILDEBEESTE (*Connochaetes taurinus*) 16, 17
WISENT (*Bison bonasus*) 141
WOLF, EUROPEAN (*Canis lupus*) 146
WOLF, NORTH AMERICAN (*Canis occidentalis*) 180

ZEBRA (*Equus quagga granti*) 13, 21, 39

PRINTED AND BOUND IN ITALY BY OFFICINE GRAFICHE A. MONDADORI IN VERONA